75p

THE COMPLETE ENGLISH POEMS
OF THOMAS GRAY

THE POETRY BOOKSHELF

General Editor: James Reeves

THOMAS GRAY
by Benjamin Wilson

THE COMPLETE
ENGLISH POEMS OF
THOMAS GRAY

*Edited with an Introduction
and Notes*

by

JAMES REEVES

HEINEMANN
LONDON

Heinemann Educational Books Ltd
LONDON EDINBURGH MELBOURNE AUCKLAND TORONTO
HONG KONG SINGAPORE KUALA LUMPUR
IBADAN NAIROBI JOHANNESBURG
NEW DELHI

ISBN 0 435 15071 5 (cased)
ISBN 0 435 15072 3 (paper)

Published by
Heinemann Educational Books Ltd
48 Charles Street, London W1X 8AH
Printed in Great Britain by Morrison & Gibb Ltd
London and Edinburgh

CONTENTS

FRAGMENTARY AND UNDATED POEMS

COMMENTARY AND NOTES 109

INDEX OF TITLES AND FIRST LINES 119

INTRODUCTION

I

THOMAS GRAY was born on 26 December 1716 in Cornhill, London, the fifth and only surviving child of Philip Gray, a scrivener, and his wife Mary. Mary and her sister Dorothy ran a business from the house, described both as a milliner's and as an India warehouse. The marriage was an unhappy one, for Gray's father was an unstable, violent man, tortured by jealousy of the women and even of their shop from whose modest profits he expected them to provide for themselves and his son. In occasional moods of savage, rather pathetic fury, he would attack his wife 'in the most inhuman manner, by beating, kicking, and punching, and with the most vile and abusive language'.[1] Dorothy Gray bore all this with fortitude for the sake of her son who grew up constitutionally weak and sensitive. He became an introspective and bookish boy, doted on by his mother and aunt, afraid of his father, and lacking all contact with children of his own age. An acute, nervous isolation was to be with him throughout nearly all his life and it is the directing energy of much that he wrote. His uncles, who were masters at Eton, resolved that he should be saved from this atmosphere, and in 1725 Gray was sent to the school where he was to pass the most idyllic days of his life.

Gray's imagination was fed at Eton by the Gothic buildings erected by Henry VI, 'the murther'd saint' as he was to call him, and by the castle nearby at Windsor. His antiquarian interests, which

[1] Mason's *Memoirs of the Life and Writings of Mr Gray* [Mason], 119.

are central in many of his works, and which he was to follow passionately throughout his life, were first roused here; and here too he first met friends with similar tastes. When he was thirteen or fourteen he became a member of what was known as the Quadruple Alliance. Horace Walpole, the Prime Minister's son, Richard West, a frail, scholarly boy, and Thomas Ashton, a somewhat more obscure figure, became his closest companions. They were precociously intelligent and sensitive boys, shunning the crowd and living in a fantasy pastoral world. Walpole described the heavily romantic atmosphere which they created for themselves in a beautiful letter to George Montague, another Etonian acquaintance:

At first I was contented with tending a visionary flock, and sighing some pastoral name to the echo of the cascade under the bridge: how happy should I have been to have had a kingdom, only for the pleasure of being driven from it, and living disguised in a humble vale. As I got farther into Virgil and *Clelia*, I found myself transported from Arcadia, to the garden of Italy, and saw Windsor Castle in no other view than the *capitoli immobile saxum* . . . I can't say I am sorry I was never quite a schoolboy; an expedition against bargemen, or a match at cricket may be very pretty things to recollect; but thank my stars, I can remember things that are very near as pretty.[2]

Here were people who would appreciate such a figure as Gray who read Virgil for pleasure and not just for lessons. They welcomed him into the clique with the name Orosmades. Gray's affection was deeply stirred and he lived with a confident, spontaneous happiness that he was later to recreate, when severed from it, in his *Ode on a Distant Prospect of Eton College*.

The period of 'the sunshine of the breast' came to its inevitible close. Gray and Ashton went up to Cambridge in 1734, to be followed a few months later by Walpole. West, more cruelly separated, was sent to Magdalen College, Oxford. Both Gray and West felt lonely. 'Absent I tread Etonian ground', wrote the latter. The years of delight were already acquiring the status of a myth. Gray, as so often in his life, lived by letters. The descriptions of

[2] Walpole's *Correspondance*, ed. W. S. Lewis, ix, 3–4.

Cambridge he sent to Walpole show an acutely critical mind turning disillusion and loneliness into a humour designed to enliven both of them. 'The Fellows are sleepy, drunken, dull, illiterate Things', he declared.[3] Peterhouse, his own college, he described as 'a thing like two Presbyterian Meeting-houses with the backside of a little Church between them'.[4] Things improved when Walpole eventually arrived, but even he wrote to West: 'there is no Quadruple Alliance: that was a happiness which I only enjoyed when you was at Eton'.[5]

In 1736 Gray came into a small legacy which allowed him to live a little like a gentleman scholar. His father's sister had died and it was found that she had left her money to Gray rather than her brother whose marriage was now threatened by divorce. In the same year it was decided that Gray should eventually adopt the law. It was not necessary to hold a degree to study at the Inner Temple, but Gray continued at Cambridge, giving up mathematics and metaphysics which he disliked, and amusing himself instead with a prolonged study of English and French poetry, to which he soon added Italian, and a thoroughly comprehensive reading of the classics. He developed a familiarity with all aspects of classical writing, and, as at Eton, became known as something of a writer of Latin poetry himself. The pattern of his future life, a life of voracious, unsupervised study, was becoming fixed. With it went a depression which he was already familiar with:

> Low spirits (he wrote to West) are my true and faithful companions; they get up with me, make journeys and returns as I do; nay, and pay me visits, and will even affect to be jocose, and force a feeble laugh with me; but most commonly we sit alone together, and are the prettiest insipid company in the world.[6]

This intense, elegant self-analysis was always to be with him, and from his letters of the period we can see him becoming increasingly

[3] *The Correspondance of Thomas Gray*, ed. Toynbee and Whibley (Corr) O.U.P. 1935, 3.   [4] *Corr.* 23–24.
[5] Quoted Ketton-Cremer, *Thomas Gray: a biography*, 14.
[6] *Corr.* 66.

self-aware. Walpole, like most young men, cured his low spirits by falling in love. For Gray it was different. In a letter that he wrote to Walpole in London we can see the humorous, but, after all, rather pained self-depreciation that was to characterize him throughout his life. We can also glimpse that half-envious, half-mocking fascination with easy aristocratic life from which he felt divorced, not only because of money, but in spirit. A note of ironic pedantry has crept in:

> I don't wonder at the new study (i.e. love) you have taken a liking to; first because it diverts your thoughts from disagreeable objects, next, because it particularly suits your Genius, and lastly, because I believe it the most excellent of all sciences, to which in proportion as the rest are subservient, so great a degree of estimation they ought to gain: would you believe it, 'tis the very thing I would wish to apply to, myself? ay! as simple as I stand here: but then the Apparatus necessary to it costs so much; nay, part of it is wholly out of one's power to procure; and then who should pare one, and burnish one? for they would have more trouble and fuss with me, than Cinderaxa's sisters had with their feet to make 'em fit for the little glass Slipper. . . . Bear I was born, and bear, I believe, I'm like to remain: consequently a little ungainly in my fondnesses, but I'll be bold to say, you shan't in a hurry meet with a more loving poor animal Creature,
>
> your faithful Creature,
>
> Bruin[7]

Gray's first three years at Cambridge came to an end, and on 29 March 1739 he and Walpole set out on the Grand Tour – that obligatory visit to Greece and Rome that was the climax to every young gentleman's education. Walpole had invited Gray to accompany him and had offered to pay his expenses, though they were to travel as equals. Gray naturally accepted. The couple idled pleasantly through France and came at last to the Alps, visiting the monastery of the Grande Chartreuse. The winding mountain road, the clouds above the hanging woods, and the cascades falling over sheer precipices, had a profound effect on both of them, particularly

[7] *Corr.* 80.

Gray. His imagination suddenly saw new boundaries and he was excited to a sense of awe such as he had never known. Some weeks later he wrote to the now ailing West:

> I own I have not, as yet, any where met with those grand and simple works of Art, that are to amaze one, and whose sight one is to be the better for: But those of Nature have astonished me beyond expression. In our little journey up to the Grande Chartreuse, I do not remember to have gone ten paces without an exclamation, that there was no restraining: Not a precipice, not a torrent, not a cliff, but is pregnant with religion and poetry. There are certain scenes that would awe an atheist into belief, without the help of other argument.[8]

'Pregnant with religion and poetry'; the phrase is significant, for Gray had glimpsed the fusion of these two in a state of great excitement, and a need for aspiration and illumination were to return to him as he developed his ideas on the nature of the poet in *The Bard* and *The Progress of Poesy*. Gray's two visits to the Grande Chartreuse were to have a crucial effect on his imagination, but for the moment he and Walpole left this exciting scenery and its secluded monks and continued on their way to Rome.

It was perhaps inevitable that two men travelling so closely and for so long should eventually be aware of friction. Besides, both Gray and Walpole were developing in rather different directions. There is a delightful picture of Walpole in carnival costume painted about this time which shows him bright-eyed, sociable, and fun-loving. He entered fully into the life of masked balls and entertainments that were provided for foreign visitors and he sported a mistress. At times he found Gray rather tedious. In Florence, the poet busied himself with a long work called *De Principiis Cogitandi*, which he never finished, and throughout the tour he filled voluminous notebooks, as he was to do for the rest of his life, with his impressions of the works in every gallery and collection and with a copy of each Latin inscription he found. 'Then I have danced, good Gods! how have I danced!'[9] wrote Walpole to West. Gray, on

[8] *Corr.* 128.
[9] Quoted Ketton-Cremer, 39.

the other hand, wrote to him from Rome of a ball at the Villa Patrizi 'where the world danced, and I sat in the corner regaling myself with iced fruits, and other pleasant rinfrescatives.'[10] It is not a very important incident, but it is symptomatic. There lies behind the phrase that feeling of a divorce from the normal, spontaneous world that is to haunt Gray's poetry from the *Ode on the Spring*, through the agonizing self-awareness in the *Sonnet on the Death of Mr Richard West*, and which is to be partly resolved in the conception of the poet in the great Pindaric Odes.

The inevitable quarrel between Gray and Walpole broke out and Gray came home alone, this time spending a little longer at the monastery of the Grande Chartreuse. Here he wrote his first masterpiece, his *Alcaic Ode*. Significantly, he is still expressing his deepest concerns in Latin. I have included it with a translation since it marks a crucial stage in Gray's development:

O Tu, severi religio loci,
Quocumque gaudes nomine (non leve
  Nativa nam certe fluenta
    Numen habet, veteresque silvas;

Praesentiorem et conspicimus Deum
Per invias rupes, fera per iuga,
  Clivosque praeruptos, sonantes
    Inter aquas, nemorumque noctem;

Quam si repostus sub trabe citrea
Fulgeret auro, et Phidiaca manu)
  Salve vocanti rite, fesso et
    Da placidam iuveni quietem.

Quod si invidendis sedibus, et frui
Fortuna sacra lege silentii
  Vetat volentem, me resorbens
    In medios violenta fluctus:

[10] *Corr.* 150.

Saltem remote des, Pater, angulo
Horas senectae ducere liberas;
  Tutumque vulgari tumultu
  Surripias, hominumque curis.

O Thou, divine spirit of this forbidding place, by whatever title pleases Thee (for certainly no mean power rules over these native streams and ancient forests; and we perceive God closer to us among pathless rocks, wild ridges and precipitous ravines, and in the thundering of waters and the darkness of the woods, than if, kept under a roof of citrus-wood, He glowed with gold even from the hand of Phidias): Hail! And if I invoke thee rightly, grant a calm repose to this weary youth.

But if Fortune forbids me, in spite of my wish, to enjoy this enviable dwelling and the scared rule of silence, sucking me back violently into the midst of the waves, then at least grant, Father, that I may pass the untroubled hours of old age in some secluded corner; and bear me off unharmed from the tumult of the crowd and the cares of men.

It is the type of work known as a Retirement Poem, and the last lines clearly look forward to 'Far from the madding crowd's ignoble strife' in the *Elegy*. The poem presents a moving portrait of an emotional solitary, aware of the intensity of revealed experience, but frightened of the abrasive, vulgarizing touch of the mass. The poet is clearly showing himself as one apart, and this is conventional enough, but it is his reason for doing so that is new. He has become a solitary explorer, aware of the life of the spirit, and as such knowing his isolation and treasuring his uniquely valuable difference. We shall see these themes again in the two Pindaric Odes, but for the moment let us compare these lines with those written by Coleridge in his *Hymn Before Sun-Rise in the Vale of Chamouni*:

Hast thou a charm to stay the morning-star
In his steep course? So long he seems to pause
On thy bald awful head, O sovran Blanc,
The Arve and Arveiron at thy base
Rave ceaselessly; but thou, most awful Form!
Risest from forth thy silent sea of pines,
How silently! Around thee and above

Deep is the air and dark, substantial, black,
An ebon mass: methinks thou piercest it,
As with a wedge! But when I look again,
It is thine own calm home, thy crystal shrine,
Thy habitation from eternity!
O dread and silent Mount! I gazed upon thee,
Till thou, still present to the bodily sense,
Didst vanish from my thought: entranced in prayer
I worshiped the Invisible alone.

The origins of the excitement are similar in both cases; but where, with Gray, we get a sense of modesty and retreat, with Coleridge we are shown the poet recalling his actual experience. Gray's is the poem of an ascetic. The sense of being inspired and transported is similar to Coleridge's, but there is no ebullience, the excitement does not strain at the language, and we come back, after all, to a certain melancholy. The passage from Coleridge is boundlessly confident because the experience is completely spontaneous and out of time. For Coleridge, to be alone is glorious for he is lost in something greater than himself; for Gray, to be alone is to be apart. His poem is more aware of everyday life, more pained.

Gray was dispirited by the London he returned to. Besides, he was now twenty-five, unqualified for a career, and beset by the feeling that he had done nothing worthy of his talents. The scholarly companionship of West was a great source of strength to him however, and, after the quarrel with Walpole, must have helped to show him where his true vocation lay. He worked on his unfinished and unstageable tragedy, *Agrippina*, a work closely modelled on Racine's *Britannicus*, a favourite play which he had seen performed in Paris. He also wrote his first major poem in English, his *Ode on the Spring*.

Johnson, in his discussion of the poem in his *Life of Gray*, thought that the Ode 'has something poetical, both in the language and the thought; but the language is too luxuriant, and the thoughts have nothing new. . . . The morality is natural but too stale; the conclusion is pretty'. In fact this rather misses the point. The poem is a revival of the old debate about the choice between the active and the contemplative life, expressed in terms of consistent irony. There is no explicit 'morality': the problems are presented dramatically and left unresolved. The 'Attic Warbler' is how the poet, 'reclined in rustic state', chooses to describe what he hears. His ensuing moralizing is deliberately stilted and accords with this conventional poeticizing of the landscape around him. In other words the presentation is deliberately ironic and delicately humorous. In the last stanza, however, he undercuts his mock-serious picture of himself by showing something real: the equal futility of his own solitary life to that of the 'insect youth'. Here the poem finishes with no conclusion drawn and only the point that death comes both to the 'sportive kind' and to the 'poor moralist' alike. The poem is a light but sophisticated one and it is a useful prelude to the *Elegy* where once again the equality of the active and contemplative lives before death are discussed, but more profoundly. Gray sent the poem to West but received no answer until his letter was returned unopened. His worst suspicions were confirmed when he read a newspaper some time later. West was dead.

II

Gray was terribly pained by West's death and with his despair came his first and most prolific period of creativity. As late as the 1760s, that is nearly twenty years after West's death, Gray's friend Norton Nichols wrote that:

> Whenever I mentioned Mr West he looked serious, & seemed to feel the affliction of a recent loss. He said that the cause of the disorder, a consumption, which brought him to an early grave was the fatal discovery which he made of the treachery of a supposed friend, & the viciousness of a mother whom he tenderly loved; this man under the mask of friendship to him & his family intrigued with his mother; & robbed him of his peace of mind, his health, & his life.[11]

[11] Norton Nichols in his *Reminiscences of Gray.*

While staying at Stoke Poges, Buckinghamshire, after West's death, Gray wrote three poems: *Ode on a Distant Prospect of Eton College*, the *Ode to Adversity*, and the poem we shall look at first, the superlative *Sonnet on the Death of Mr Richard West*.

It is the diction of this poem that has caused the greatest amount of comment, stimulated, of course, by Wordsworth's adverse criticism of it in the Preface to the *Lyrical Ballads*. Before discussing this, however, it is necessary to show the cruel central paradox of the poem: the fact that the poet's grief could only be understood by the dead friend for whom he weeps. From Gray's sense of desolation, of the impotence of grief, comes his feeling of hopeless isolation. The poem is one of profound despair. No consolation is offered as it is in *Lycidas*. Instead, the most intense language, raised, in the last two lines, to the level of a bitter and almost Metaphysical wit, maintains a tightness of form which is a measure of the poet's noble strength. The literary origins of the poem, which in no way devalue Gray's terrible clarity of expression, are, ironically, a poem by West himself, which was influenced in its turn by a passage from one of Pope's last letters:

> The morning after my Exit, the sun will rise as bright as ever, the flowers smell as sweet, the plants spring as green, the world will proceed in its old course, people will laugh as heartily, and marry as fast as they were us'd to do.

The diction of the poem has been widely misunderstood. Wordsworth claimed that only lines 6–8 and 13–14 had 'any value', a criticism that Hopkins called 'rude at best'. These lines are of course those written in 'a selection of the language really used by men'. The rest, many of which contain borrowed phrases, have been found dull and are variously excused. In fact, if the sonnet is read with attention to the sound, and Gray's ear was exquisitely refined, it will be realized that the melody of the vowel sounds is particularly rich. The images are somewhat stereotyped, it is true, but the extent of this can be exaggerated, and Professor Tillotson is partly right when he says Gray uses them ironically to show up the hollow joy of other poets compared to his own grief. It must also be remembered that Gray and his audience were used to the employment of allusions to emphasize the richness of tradition. This is different from mere plagiarizing. To be cut off from the normal association of poetic diction, as Gray's partly ironic use suggests, furthers his sense of desolation. Gray is thus using again, but in a more complex way, the figure of the poet seeing the world through the language he uses, which we found in the *Ode on the Spring*. If, as I suggest, we listen to the sound of these lines, then a sense of richness still comes across, the tension between what the ear hears and the mind reads deepens our awareness of the situation, and the sparseness of the lines that follow is all the more terrible:

> My lonely anguish melts no heart but mine;
> And in my breast the imperfect joys expire.

When we have grasped this paradox between sound and meaning, then we can appreciate the effect of the sestet where the theme of teeming nature and the isolated poet is repeated in a variation. A careful aural reading will show that there are several deliberate half-rhymes with words in the octave to emphasize this repetition. Now the poet shows that what appears as the indifference of nature affects him alone. Happier men *are* cheered, the fields are rejuvenated for a purpose, and the birds no longer sing in vain. Normal life pursues its more or less happy course, and Gray's loneliness is made the more painful by the absence of the comfort granted to others. He is truly exiled by his grief. Though the birds now sing to rouse each other's love, his loved friend is dead. The comparison provides the bitterest irony of all:

> I fruitless mourn to him that cannot hear,
> And weep the more because I weep in vain.

This is a deeply moving and profoundly personal poem. Gray did not publish it in his lifetime.

A lack of spontaneous joy almost inevitably leads to an idealization of childhood and this is what we find in the *Ode on a Distant*

Prospect of Eton College. Having apparently lost his two greatest friends, being financially insecure, and uncertain as to his future, Gray's time at Eton now took on an almost prelapsarian innocence. In fact the *Ode* does not closely resemble Gray's own experience; as always in his poetry the movement is away from the purely subjective to the type – even the sonnet is bare of personal anecdote – and the Virgilian musings of the Quadruple Alliance have no place here. A contemporary records that Walpole said that 'Gray was never a boy', and his descriptions of the games are undoubtedly a little ironic. However, these passages, as well as the historical references at the opening, are commonplaces of the genre known as the Topographical Poem, and this is what the *Ode* at first appears to be. Gray's originality lies in his use of nostalgia, of time past and present, to create a picture of innocence and experience. As in the *Alcaic Code* and many later works, particularly of course the *Elegy*, Gray presents his view of the world with a special emphasis on Time. With this comes both his melancholy and later his need to escape from Time's effects. The timeless spontaneity of childhood thus became something as infinitely precious to Gray as it was to Wordsworth, and the similarities between this work and the *Ode: Intimations of Immortality from Recollections of Early Childhood* are obvious. But where, with Wordsworth, a partial redemption from Time is achieved through memory, with Gray, on the other hand, Time is only progressive and hence the stoic epigraph: 'I am a man; sufficient excuse for being unhappy'. The *Eton Ode* is deeply pessimistic, but in the companion poem, the *Ode to Adversity*, the picture of Time the Destroyer is modified. The epigraph from the *Agamemnon* of Aeschylus reads: 'Zeus, who leadeth mortals in the way of understanding, Zeus, who hath established as a fixed ordinance that wisdom comes by suffering'. What the poem presents is the gradual education of the heart by the pain that is seen as inevitable in the previous work. Gray put the argument of the poem in a letter he wrote to a friend some four years later:

... our Imperfections may at least excuse, & perhaps recommend us to one another: methinks I can readily pardon Sickness & Age & Vexation for all the Depredations they make within & without, when I think they make us better Friends & better Men, wch I am persuaded is often the Case.[12]

With Wordsworth, the joys and fears of the heart lead him to the state where:

> . . . the meanest flower that blows can give
> Thoughts that do often lie too deep for tears.

In other words the revelation is to the individual – to the 'egotistical sublime' – and not to a man more conscious of society. It is partly this consciousness that keeps Gray on the threshold of Romanticism, and the problem of the relation of the artist to society was to occupy him increasingly. For the moment however he returned to Cambridge in the mood of ironical resignation expressed in his *Hymn to Ignorance*.

III

It is not known exactly when Gray began his *Elegy Written in a Country Churchyard*, but it is generally reckoned to have been some time after West's death. As with many of his later poems, Gray worked at the *Elegy* for a considerable period, and he sent the completed manuscript to Walpole on 12 June 1750. The breach between them had now been healed, and Walpole enthusiastically sent copies of the poem to his friends. Gray, as we shall see, was far from pleased by this and it led to considerable embarrassment.

The *Elegy* is by far the finest example of a genre that was particularly popular in the eighteenth century: the Retirement Poem that was also a meditation on death. The literature behind the form, both classical and biblical, is enormous, but what we find in the eighteenth century is a particular emphasis on melancholy and a sometimes morbid fascination with corpses and the Last Judgement. The works

[12] *Corr.* 248.

differ from their seventeenth-century models mainly by a lack of intellectual vigour and a sterility of language. The immediate precursors of the *Elegy* are such works as Blair's *The Grave*, Parnell's *Night Piece on Death*, and Young's voluminous *Night Thoughts* which gave this now almost forgotten poet an international reputation. Such works show a connection between nature and the poet's melancholy which was strongly influenced by Milton's *Il Penseroso*. However, we must avoid confusing the word melancholy with the idea of mere depression. Burton defines it in his *Anatomy of Melancholy* as 'a kind of dotage without a fever, having for [its] ordinary companions, fear and sadness, without any apparent occasion'. It came to be looked on as a fruitful state, and the elegy, its natural form, 'by presenting suitable ideas, has discovered sweets in melancholy, which we could not find in mirth; and has led us with success to the dusty urn, when we could draw no pleasure from the sparkling bowl'. Such is Shenstone's description, and in his own mediocre works we find that melancholy and precise self-analysis with which Gray had filled his correspondence – though Gray nearly always adds a note of ironic humour. Burton had shown that the solitary scholar was particularly prone to melancholy, and Gray now brought his own passion and craftsmanship to bear.

The *Elegy* exists in two distinct versions. The first and shorter one, which Gray later rejected, had these four stanzas as a conclusion after line 72:

> The thoughtless World to Majesty may bow
> Exalt the brave, & idolize Success
> But more to Innocence their Safety owe
> Than Power and Genius e'er conspired to bless

> And thou, who mindful of the unhonour'd Dead
> Dost in these Notes their artless Tale relate
> By Night & lonely Contemplation led
> To linger in the gloomy Walks of Fate

> Hark the sacred Calm, that broods around
> Bids ev'ry fierce tumultuous Passion cease
> In still small Accents whisp'ring from the Ground
> A grateful Earnest of eternal Peace
>
> No more with Reason and thyself at strife;
> Give anxious Cares and endless Wishes room
> But thro' the cool sequester'd Vale of Life
> Pursue the silent Tenour of thy Doom.

The first version is a simple but exquisite exercise in Christian stoicism. The scene is set, and then, in the middle section, the lives of the villagers are described. If they have been deprived of opportunity, Gray writes, they have also been protected from great crime. The poem closes with the poet's return to himself and his decision to share the villagers' obscure existence rather than expose himself to the snares of the world. There is a tone of resignation and a calm hope in the world to come. The poem is perfectly balanced and simple. Ultimately, perhaps, it was too simple. It could not adequately suggest Gray's predicament, and his second version, the commonly known one, is concerned with exposing and then resolving his special position as a poet in terms of his philosophy.

The changes Gray made have led to some unnecessarily obtuse readings of the poem. In fact it presents an important and perfectly clear argument. The poem is built up on contrasts throughout. The contrast between the rustics and the great world leads to the poet's choice of obscurity, but simple renunciation is not enough. Just as 'from the tomb the voice of nature cries', so the pessimism of renunciation obscures the delight of life and the value of our feelings. Unobtrusively, and therefore all the more powerfully, Gray juxtaposes his vivid images of life and death. First of all we see the poet in the evening churchyard with its delicately macabre atmosphere:

> . . . from yonder ivy-mantled tower
> The moping owl does to the moon complain

> Of such as, wandering near her secret bower,
> Molest her ancient solitary reign.

And then, offset by the deep melancholy of the last line, we are shown fresh, morning nature:

> The breezy call of incense-breathing morn,
> The swallow twittering from the straw-built shed,
> The cock's shrill clarion or the echoing horn,
> No more shall rouse them from their lowly bed.

There is a glory that it is difficult to leave behind, and in recognizing this we crave a memorial as some defence against Time:

> For who to dumb Forgetfulness a prey,
> This pleasing anxious being e'er resigned,
> Left the warm precincts of the cheerful day,
> Nor cast one longing lingering look behind?

It is partly Gray's acceptance of this problem that makes him superior to the other 'graveyard poets'. He refuses to allow his resignation to be purely negative, and as a result human feeling comes to the fore. All men, both rich and poor, both the active and those who have retired from the world are equal before death, says Gray, as he did in the *Ode to the Spring*, but now we feel a genuine sympathy for both, uncluttered by the moralist's rhetoric. He sees the need for some memorial, and the 'storied urn' and 'animated bust', treated more disparagingly in the earlier stanzas, now become tinged with pathos. Indeed, in these earlier stanzas, there had been some bitter irony. An 'animated bust' on a tomb is itself ironical, and this is deepened by the mention of the 'fleeting breath' which is what is truly animating, while the second two lines of this stanza, with their deliberate opposition of honour and flattery – the good and the bad in the public world – show that both are unable to 'soothe the dull cold ear of death' which thus becomes all the more ruthless. It is already clear that under the smooth and measured language of the *Elegy* there is a complex and consistent, sometimes ironic, juxtaposition of thought and feeling. This is increased by the introduction of the idea of 'knowledge' in line 49. Knowledge is almost immediately associated with the knowledge of evil. The rustics have been deprived of this, though the idea that, given the chance, they *would* 'wade through slaughter to a throne' is implicit; and though 'their sober wishes never learn'd to stray' – this verb is most important here, Gray changed it from the weaker 'know' to emphasize his point – yet their fields are no Eden and the poem is far from a sentimental pastoral escape such as is too common in eighteenth-century poetry:

> Chill Penury repressed their noble rage,
> And froze the genial current of the soul.

Empson has criticized the following stanza (lines 53–56) for seducing the reader into thinking that 'we ought to accept the injustice of society as we do the inevitability of death'. To a certain extent he is right. Gray is not moved to change the status quo, and we have seen why; what he does do, however, is elect to join the rustics, accepting their life and his own implicit ideas of the impossibility of change.

It is true that 'the paths of glory lead but to the grave', as does that of the ploughman, but there is a third type of man, a man more knowledgeable than the ploughman and so able to see his worth as well as the emptiness of worldly success by which he could have been tempted – this is the man of feeling, the poet. The difficulty with interpretation has arisen with lines 93–96, but this is removed if we remember that the poem is a soliloquy among the tombs. After the high note sounded by lines 91–92, it is dramatically appropriate that the speaker should return to himself and address his image of himself in the second person. The poet, who, at the end of the first stanza, has shown himself as someone special and apart, now returns to discuss his place in the world. The lines about the 'mute inglorious Milton' take on a new dimension. The poet *is* knowledgeable and he is *not* mute; thus his problem is to preserve his integrity in a world where others have made careers from the remnants of their sensibility by heaping:

> . . . the shrine of Luxury and Pride
> With incense kindled at the Muse's flame.

This was very much the state of poetry in Gray's time, and he would have none of it. The Laureateship had become a farcical post and he was later to decline it. We have seen already how he thought that his sensibility set him apart, and by having a 'hoary-headed swain' recount his story with a mixture of awe and incomprehension, this idea of the 'otherness' of the true poet, and of his divorce from the venal and urbane society of eighteenth-century London, comes across most powerfully. The poet is presented as a strange and ethereal creature:

> Oft have we seen him at the peep of dawn
> Brushing with hasty steps the dews away
> To meet the sun upon the upland lawn.
>
> There at the foot of yonder nodding beech
> That wreathes its old fantastic roots so high,
> His listless length at noontide would he stretch,
> And pore upon the brook that babbles by.

It has been pointed out that these lines resemble the description of Jaques in *As You Like It*, and Gray was certainly aware of this, but they are perhaps closer to some lines in Dryden's *All For Love* where Anthony describes himself in an identical setting and as having 'turn'd wild' and become:

> . . . a commoner of nature;
> Of all forsaken and forsaking all.

Gray sees himself as a similarly strange creature, to be pitied (as much as admired) for his acute sensibility, one who roves the countryside 'mutt'ring his wayward fancies' alone. He knew that he had to go by this way of inspiration. For this – though he greatly admired the poem – Dr Johnson never forgave Gray.

> . . . he had a notion not very peculiar, that he could not write but at certain times, or at happy moments; a fantastic foppery, to which my kindness for a man of learning and of virtue wishes him to have been superior.

By making the poet strange and unsociable, poetry becomes an exclusively private activity, and it is possible to see how the esoteric Pindaric Odes developed out of this attitude. The poet has been singled out. Unlike the rustics:

> Fair Science frowned not on his humble birth,
> And Melancholy marked him for her own.

Knowledge, properly seen, becomes something valuable, though a burden and a possible snare, and the melancholy that goes with it produces a rare sensibility. However, the poetry engendered is not something to be thrown to the crowd in the hope of being remembered. The poet elects the obscurity of the churchyard, and his epitaph, his final poem, emphasizes that he wishes to be remembered only for his human qualities. There is no mention of art as a defence against time, save implicitly in his epitaph, which describes his virtues as a man, and these are modestly stated in comparison to the facile eulogies so common at the time. God knows everything, and it is to him, in 'trembling hope', that the poet consigns his merits and frailties. A unique picture of a poet's special nature and his integrity has been drawn in a Retirement Poem which is neither sentimental nor nihilistic and which shows him as a heroic and profoundly human figure.

Walpole, as we have seen, immediately circulated copies of the *Elegy*, and it fell into the hands of the publishers of the rather third-rate *Magazine of Magazines*. To avoid publishing in this, Gray wrote to Walpole: 'As you have brought me into a little Sort of Distress, you must assist me, I believe, to get out of it, as well as I can.'[13] The *Elegy* was duly printed, anonymously, in a sixpenny pamphlet. The author did not remain unknown for long, despite his real desire, implicit in the poem, for obscurity. Gray had genuinely written the poem for himself and a few friends. The *Elegy* was a remarkable success, however, and was frequently reprinted, imitated and translated. This immediate fame deeply embarrassed Gray, yet he carefully listed the various editions the poem went through and no doubt his private pleasure was considerable. A fundamentally lonely man, his popularity must have fascinated him, and at times he was deliberately coy about his authorship of the work. Nevertheless, as we shall see when we come to the Pindaric Odes, there was a deep sincerity underlying Gray's ambiguous relations with the public.

IV

Gray had now returned to Cambridge. Apart from a two-year period in London, where much of his time was spent at the British Museum, he was to pass the rest of his life at the University. His vacations were spent with friends or visiting historic monuments around the country. In his Notebooks he has left many vivid impressions of what he saw on these travels. In 1751, at Walpole's insistence, *Designs by Mr R. Bentley for Six Poems by Mr T. Gray* was issued. Gray's reluctance to appear as a public poet is reflected in the title and also in his *Stanzas to Mr Bentley*. His poems, he decided, were 'only subordinate and explanatory to the drawings'.[14] These are very charming, and the volume has been called 'the most graceful monument to Gothic Rococo'. Four of the poems had already appeared, and the reception of the book mattered little to Gray. His mother had died, and the inscription he placed on her tombstone reads: 'The careful tender mother of many children, one of whom alone had the misfortune to survive her'.

[13] *Corr.* 341–2.
[14] *Corr.* 371.

How did Gray spend his time in Cambridge, which he described as being ruled by 'that ineffable Octogrammaton the Power of LAZINESS'?[15]

He had a small, close circle of friends, men who appreciated the power of feeling and intellect that surged under his increasingly strange outward character. He wrote his poems very slowly and at infrequent intervals, but he passed the long days accumulating an extraordinary range of knowledge, and his Notebooks are full of writings on history, botany, early English poetry – a subject that was to become of great importance – the classics, and the most detailed studies of metre and poetic form. These studies were pursued in fantastic detail. 'He was, in fact, taking the whole of the ancient world for his province', writes Ketton Cremer, 'and his reading and note-taking ranged from the sublimities of philosophy and poetry to the smallest details of domestic life – the wines and vineyards of the Greeks and Romans, their vehicles and furniture, food and medicine, clothing and footgear and pottery.' These Notebooks are a moving sight when we consider the author of the *Elegy*. They are so clearly a bulwark against despair. 'To find oneself business is the great art of life', Gray wrote, and again, 'to be employed is to be happy'.[16] One is reminded of Pascal's statement: 'If ours were a condition of true content, we should need no form of amusement to keep us from thinking of it.'

This desperate fastidiousness was reflected in Gray's public personality, though he increasingly kept to his rooms to nurse his gout and lassitude. There can be little doubt that he was homosexual, and both his faith and the law forbade him to be open about this. Henry Tuthill, whose place at Pembroke Gray had helped to secure, was discharged from his duties for being 'under violent suspicion of having been guilty of great enormities'. What these were is pretty clear from the embarrassment which the incident caused. There is a direction in Gray's will that his executors should 'apply the sum of two hundred pounds to the use of a charity, which I have already

[15] *Corr.* 223.
[16] Quoted Ketton-Cremer, 213.

informed them of' and this may well concern the unfortunate man. Gray himself was frequently described as affected and even effeminate, and I think it helps us to a deeper understanding of the man if we recognize this side of his nature. It explains the agonies of platonic ardour which he suffered, near the end of his life, for the fascinating young Swiss named Bonstetten. However, Gray's sensuality was always denied fulfilment. He deliberately immersed himself in his work and maintained a precision in every detail of his life to save himself from the flabbiness of impotent despair. The High Table might laugh at his carefully tended window-boxes and apricot marmalade, but he was indifferent to people he knew were inferior, and he was highly valued by those he honoured with his friendship. In his letters to them there is a wonderful tenderness and humour. The man who made notes on early Welsh poetry and advised a friend to obtain Bay Salt for *pot pourri* in London rather than Cambridge, 'where under the name of Bay Salt they sell a whitish kind of salt, that will never do for our Purpose, and will spoil all',[17] lived under a titanic self-restraint which explains, and, if necessary, excuses, his vitriolic satires. There are few of them and they have been too neglected, but *The Candidate*, a swingeing attack on academic ambition in a corrupt university, is as fine as any of the period. Gray sees the whole incident as ultimately pathetic.

It is clear from the *Elegy* that Gray was deeply interested in the problems of education. The conditions under which it thrived and its place in society are the subject of his uncompleted work *The Alliance of Education and Government*. Gray's opinion of the didactic poem was always uncertain. He had a detailed knowledge of Lucretius, but he knew that his own talents were primarily lyrical. 'The true Lyric style,' he wrote, 'with all its flights of fancy, ornaments & heightening of expression, & harmony of sound, is in its nature superior to every other style'.[18] Temperamentally, he was driven to side with Longinus and his essay *On The Sublime* in the eighteenth-century debate between this critic's ideas and the Aristotelian rules. Walter Bate writes:

[17] Quoted Ketton-Cremer, 199.   [18] *Corr.* 608.

The urging by Longinus of the psychological and emotional elements in the creation and understanding of art, his assumption that art should transport as well as persuade, and his emphasis upon boldness and grandeur of conception and upon a capacity for the pathetic – that is to say, for the raising of the passions – as all important and inherent aesthetic gifts, served as something of an authoritative rallying centre for the defence of a subjective and emotional taste.[19]

This uncertainty of Gray's may have been one reason for the poem's being unfinished. Another is the fact that Montesquieu, in his *L'Esprit des Loix*, 'had forestalled some of his best thoughts', as Mason wrote. These thoughts were primarily about the effect of the environment on national character.

The relationship between the *Elegy* and the ideas in this poem, the full title of which Mason gives as *The Necessary Alliance Between A Good Form Of Government And A Mode Of Education, In Order To Produce The Happiness Of Mankind*, appears at first ambiguous. The opening lines declare that men without education are like sickly plants in a barren soil, yet in the *Elegy* such men are presented as almost fortunate. This paradox is resolved, I think, if we consider that in the *Elegy*, a more personal poem, Gray was stressing the pessimistic side of a favourite passage of his in the sixth book of Plato's *Republic*, which he paraphrased thus in his Notebook:

... those Excellencies & Endowments required to form a Mind suscept-ible of true Philosophy; as a quick & retentive Understanding, a high spirit, & a natural Greatness, & Simplicity of Soul (more particularly, if attended with what the World calls Blessings: Opulence, Birth & Beauty of Person) are the most likely to draw off the Youth that possesses them, from that very Pursuit they were design'd for: and lighting (as he expresses it) in an improper Soil, that is, corrupted by a bad Education, & ill-regulated Government become the readier Instruments of Mischief to Mankind, by so much more, as Nature meant them for their Good. For every extraordinary wickedness, every action superlatively unjust is the Product of a vigorous Spirit ill-nurtured. . . .

The Alliance of Education and Government, however, sets out to show

[19] Walter J. Bate, *From Classic to Romantic*, Camb. Mass., 1946, 46–47.

the ideal and therefore generalized rules of perfection: the optimistic potential expressed in this quotation. Gray, in fact, did not get very far with this. In the *Elegy*, written about the same time, fame, which should be reserved for Plato's youth, is implicitly linked to the vanity of the 'storied urn or animated bust', and the *Epitaph* of the 'youth to fortune and to fame unknown' is a deliberately modest attempt to set out his human virtues – the sense of love and wonder in the 'swain' is equally important. Integrity, Gray implies, must quietly stand apart from the world as it now is. In an ideal society, however, a sincere and uncorrupted fame would serve the same purpose as the *Epitaph*, but it would be beneficial to a wider range of people who would be as appreciative as the 'swain', but more learned. We find this passage in the Notebooks:

Many are the uses of good fame to a generous mind: it extends our existence and example into future ages; continues and propogates virtue, which would otherwise be as short-lived as our frame; and prevents the prevalence of vice in a generation more corrupt than our own. It is impossible to conquer that natural desire we have of being remembered; even criminal ambition and avarice, the most selfish of all passions, would wish to leave a name behind them.

The *Elegy*, fortunately, is the completed poem, and in it we find the love and pathos of the involvement of a man with these ideals in a fallen world.

We have seen some of the ideas with which Gray filled his Notebooks. What were the ideas that he was formulating on poetry, and in particular on technique? We know he thought that poetry, modern poetry at any rate, 'implies at least a liberal education, a degree of literature, & various knowledge',[20] and we have seen too that his ear was acutely sensitive. He wrote: 'There is . . . a *toute ensemble* of sound, as well of sense, in poetical composition necessary to its perfection. What has gone before still dwells upon the ear, and insensibly harmonizes with the present tone, as in that succession of fleeting notes which is called Melody'.[21] His choice of words was

[20] *Corr.* 811.
[21] Mason's ed., *Poems of Mr Gray*, 87.

clearly of extreme importance, and his often quoted remark that 'the language of the age is never the language of poetry'[22] is frequently used to support Wordsworth's view that Gray had 'attempted to widen the space of separation betwixt Prose and Metrical composition, and was more than any other man curiously elaborate in the structure of his own poetic diction'. Wordsworth's prose itself is far from direct, and it is often forgotten that Gray's statement was written at the outset of his career and about dramatic verse. In 1747 he wrote to Walpole that *Agrippina* was written 'all in figures and mere poetry, instead of nature and the language of real passion'.[23] Gray, we know, often used deliberately poetic diction for an effect other than rhetoric, and his poems as a whole show a continuous experimentation with language. This is so with any true poet. For Gray, style and content must be one. This is the classical viewpoint. As a result, high thoughts need a careful choice of words. Many contemporary readers, however, considered his diction idiosyncratic as it sometimes is, though usually with a purpose. Johnson declared that it was barely grammatical, and he found the phrase 'gales redolent with joy and youth' in the *Eton College Ode* intolerable. Gray believed that colloquialisms could not express high passion. This does not mean that he did not know the power of simplicity. The *Sonnet* shows that he did, but everyday words could best be used for comic poems, as in this stanza from *A Long Story*:

> The trembling family they daunt,
> They flirt, they sing, they laugh, they tattle,
> Rummage his mother, pinch his aunt,
> And upstairs in a whirlwind rattle.

This is Gray's description of two female admirers of his work hunting him down. In his *Ode on the Death of a Favourite Cat, Drowned in a Tub of Gold Fishes*, a superb *jeu d'esprit* suggested by Walpole, Gray uses a deliberately mock-heroic diction combined

[22] *Corr.* 192–3.
[23] *Corr.* 262.

with the moralistic animal fable. This allows him some excellent
effects:

> The hapless nymph with wonder saw:
> A whisker first and then a claw,
>   With many an ardent wish,
> She stretched in vain to reach the prize.
> What female heart can gold despise?
>   What cat's averse to fish?

There is an intelligence, an ironic humour in the poem which is
prevented from being merely whimsical by its subject, but this, by
the way it is expressed, becomes itself almost humorous.

We have seen from the trouble he had with his unfinished
didactic poems that Gray was uneasy about passages of thought in
his verse that were unassimilated into either action or mood. Yet,
if he believed in the superiority of imagination, he was insistent
upon unity of feeling in a poem. The man who wrote 'rules are
but chains, good for little, except when one can break through
them',[24] was far from advocating a sort of *vers libre*, which is
virtually what a misunderstanding of Pindar's technique had led to
among most earlier imitators of his Odes. The imagination, in
Gray's practice, was to be kept from flabbiness by an absolute
precision of expression. His friend Mason wrote that his

> . . . conceptions, as well as his manner of disposing them, were so
> singularly exact, that he had seldom occasion to make many, except
> verbal emendations, after he had first committed his lines to paper. It
> was never his method to sketch his general design in careless verse, he
> always finished as he proceeded; this, tho' it made his execution slow,
> made his compositions more perfect.[25]

It was under this tension between ardour and clarity of expression
that the two great Pindaric Odes were written, at those rare
moments of excitement of which Gray could say: 'I felt myself
the bard'.[26]

[24] *Corr.* 1169.
[25] Mason, 233–4.
[26] *Corr.* 1290.

V

The Pindaric Ode, so called, was introduced into English poetry by Cowley in his *Pindarique Odes* of 1656, and was later taken up by Dryden in his *Song for St Cecilia's Day* and *Alexander's Feast*. The apparently loose structure and the variety of rhythm and rhyme schemes that it allowed were a welcome relief from the tyranny of the heroic couplet. Here was a form, sanctioned by antiquity, which seemed to allow a virtually free expression of ecstatic feelings. In fact, as Congreve was to point out, Pindar's odes are rigorously disciplined and highly esoteric. There is in them precisely that tension between rigidity of form and the flight of a learned imagination which would appeal to Gray. In his Notebooks we find a detailed analysis of many of the passages from Pindar he was later to imitate in his own odes. Gray was the first major English poet to fully understand and consciously apply Pindar's technique. 'In addition', writes Roger Lonsdale, in his superbly scholarly edition of the poet, 'Gray attempted to capture the manner of Pindar's odes by imitating the highly allusive and concise narrative technique and the swift transition from one topic to another which characterize them'. The basic form, but not the only one, is sets of three stanzas or triads, the stanzas being called the strophe, the antistrophe and the epode. The rhyme scheme of the strophe and the antistrophe must be identical though the epode may vary. However, the pattern established in the first triad must be duplicated exactly in the succeeding ones. The form is very far from being free, but it allows for a great variety of metre, and it is a measure of Gray's craftsmanship to see the different moods he can convey in the repeated patterns.

Both *The Bard* and *The Progress of Poesy* are, as the title of the latter work indicates, versions of the Progress Poem genre. This is a familiar eighteenth-century pattern, and the form usually adopted is a description of the flight of Liberty, and with her the liberal arts and sciences, from Greece to Rome, through Renaissance Italy to

England. In other words they are usually patriotic pieces designed to exalt the greatness of Britain. Collins' *Ode to Liberty* is a good example. However, *The Progress of Poesy* is far from confident about the state of poetry in England.

Gray's epigraph to the poem is taken from the second of the *Olympian Odes* of Pindar, and a translation of the full passage reads:

> Full many a swift arrow have I beneath mine arm, within my quiver, many an arrow that is vocal to the wise; but for the crowd they need interpreters. The true poet is he who knoweth much by gift of nature, but they that have only learned the lore of song, and are turbulent and intemperate of tongue, like a pair of crows, chatter in vain against the godlike bird of Zeus.

This passage is consciously adapted at the end of the poem to present, once again, Gray's especial predicament. The poem is a difficult one – 'vocal to the intelligent alone' was Gray's translation of the epigraph – and it is easiest to describe it systematically.

In the notes which Gray reluctantly added to the edition of the poem published in 1768 he says of the first strophe:

> The various sources of poetry, which gives life and lustre to all it touches, are here described; its quiet majestic progress enriching every subject (otherwise dry and barren) with a pomp of diction and luxuriant harmony of numbers; and its more rapid and irresistible course, when swoln and hurried away by the conflict of tumultuous passions.

Throughout the first triad we are shown the almost magical power of poetry to bring the world into harmony. Its association with nature, its ability to make

> the sullen Cares
> And frantic Passions hear thy soft control

and then, in the glorious epode, its association with dance, all make poetry appear as something elementally powerful and yet sophisticated. This feeling of joy and exultation is achieved through a freshness of expression and an exciting variety of ideas. The opening image of awakening to rapture gives a feeling of renewal that is carried over to the second triad where we are told that:

> To compensate the real and imaginary ills of life, the Muse was given to Mankind by the same Providence that sends the Day and its cheerful presence to dispel the gloom and terrors of the Night.

The conscious echo of Milton's 'And justify the ways of God to man' in line 47 emphasizes again the divine and essentially beneficent power of poetry.

We have seen already that Gray was eagerly pursuing his researches into Celtic poetry in his Notebooks. Later he was to produce a number of translations which were to have a crucial effect on European Romanticism. The gods of Greece and Rome were losing their imaginative appeal. They were too familiar from yards of plaster friezes and painted ceilings. On the other hand, a scholarly interest was now being taken in 'primitive' poetry from lands as far apart as Wales and Peru, and Bishop Percy was reviving the study of the ballad. The impetus given to this by Gray's interest, the interest of a renowned scholar, was considerable. We have seen that he recognized the absolute necessity of inspiration, and *The Progress of Poesy* itself repeats this idea. We have seen too how stimulated he was by the wildness of nature. In an age of mannered versifying a great poet recognized the merit of apparently barbaric productions. For Gray, his enthusiasm showed the 'extensive influence of poetic Genius over the remotest and most uncivilized nations: its connection with liberty, and the virtues that naturally attend on it'. Poetry expresses joy and freedom and these are seen as redemptive. There is a sincerity in the verse which raises it above the level of similar exercises. There is a feeling of faith in joy which is crucial when we come to the final epode. The progress of this regenerative enthusiasm from Greece to England closes the second triad.

The strophe of the third triad is devoted to Shakespeare, a fact that a number of readers did not recognize in the first, unannotated edition. The fact that he is presented as a child receiving his inspiration directly from the goddess of nature emphasizes the essentially spiritual nature of poetry. He is placed after the classic writers whose rules he had so successfully ignored. The implicit idea is that the rules were made for poetry, not poetry for the rules and that as a consequence Shakespeare knew the freedom of the spirit which unites him to the ancients. The antistrophe celebrates Milton and Dryden who likewise knew 'the fields of glory'.

What Gray has been saying is that poetry expresses, and is fostered by, a largeness of spirit. This is reflected in the social institutions of the time, but these are not explicitly identified with democracy, only with the 'lofty spirit' that Rome eventually lost. It is a confident feeling for man's potential that produces great art. The pessimism of the close of *The Dunciad* expresses Pope's fear that this feeling is being lost. The final epode of *The Progress of Poesy* is more complex and essentially optimistic:

> Hark, his hands the lyre explore!
> Bright-eyed Fancy hovering o'er
> Scatters from her pictured urn
> Thoughts that breathe and words that burn.
> But ah! 'tis heard no more——
> Oh! lyre divine, what daring spirit
> Wakes thee now? Though he inherit
> Nor the pride nor ample pinion,
> That the Theban eagle bear
> Sailing with supreme dominion
> Through the azure deep of air:
> Yet oft before his infant eyes would run
> Such forms as glitter in the Muse's ray
> With orient hues, unborrowed of the sun:
> Yet shall he mount and keep his distant way
> Beyond the limits of a vulgar fate,
> Beneath the Good how far – but far above the Great.

The fifth line of the epode wonderfully expresses the awful silence that marks the end of a great culture. One is reminded of these lines from the *Pervigilium Veneris*, that late masterpiece of the ancient world:

> perdidi musam tacendo, nec me Apollo respicit:
> sic Amyclas, cum tacerent, perditit silentium.

> (I lost the muse in silence, nor does Apollo regard me
> any more: so Amyclae, being mute, perished by silence.)

But Gray now considers himself. He will not perish by silence, for in his childhood he saw 'Such forms as glitter in the Muse's ray'. One is reminded of what he said about Shakespeare. It is tempting too to recall Wordsworth's lines about his knowing in his boyhood 'Gleams like the flashing of a shield'. But literature is always predictable through hindsight. Gray declares that he will go his own 'distant way' – the way of private inspiration. Yet the close of the Ode is a tissue of ironies that perfectly express his predicament. If he says he will explore alone like Pindar, yet it is Pindar's imagery he uses to say so, and also to say that he cannot go as far. If what he has seen in childhood is 'unborrowed of the sun', in other words original experience not seen through other men's works, then the image is a reminiscence of Virgil's: *nec fratris radiis obnoxia surgere Luna* (nor does the moon rise under debt to her brother's rays). The last lines, save for the superb satire of his contemporaries' ambition, are an adaptation of Horace. Gray is confident that he 'knoweth much by gift of nature', enough to make him one apart as we saw in the *Elegy*, and this state he now believes is the necessary condition for a poet. In recognizing that he is not a truly great poet, but that he *is*, nonetheless, a poet, and one who will preserve his integrity, he has had to use the words of those he admires. 'These fragments', he implies, 'I have shored against my ruins.'

We know that throughout his life Gray was deeply impressed by mountains, and this fragment of a letter gives something of the personal background to the scene created in the second of his Pindaric odes, *The Bard*:

> The Lowlands are worth seeing once, but the Mountains are extatic, & ought to be visited in pilgrimage once a year. None but those monstrous creatures of God know how to join so much beauty with so much horror.[27]

This last sentence contains a profoundly Romantic idea. In Shelley's *On The Medusa Of Leonardo Da Vinci In The Florentine Gallery* we find the line: 'Its horror and its beauty are divine'. Walpole was writing his Gothic horror-story *The Castle of Otranto*. A combination of enthusiasm and scholarship was bringing the superficially similar Saxon and Medieval worlds into this common imaginative pool. Gray's translations from the Norse and Celtic were to be crucial in this for, although his own productions were few in number, the association of the author of the *Elegy* gave the Celtic revival great impetus, and Gray's enthusiastic support of Macpherson caused the latter to write his *Ossian*. Gray may have guessed that this Celtic hero was entirely spurious. But he admired this now forgotten work, and even Napoleon chose to be ranked with its hero. The enormous influence of *Ossian*, particularly on the continent, was out of all proportion to its literary merit. It was, however, a vital catalyst.

Gray declared himself to be '*extasié* with their infinite beauty'[28] when he read Macpherson's first works, and he set about his own translations which appear to have been taken from Latin transcriptions. I think it is easy to see why the 'delicate Mr Gray' as he was called was so excited by writing such lines as:

> See the grisly texture grow,
> ('Tis of human entrails made,)
> And the weights that play below,
> Each a gasping warrior's head.

Solitary platonic ardour produces its own reactions. It is true that literature was begging for new sources, but these can only be found in the psyche, however much we choose to explain new

[27] *Corr.* 899.
[28] *Corr.* 680.

movements as 'trends'. Here, in part at least, are the origins of that sado-masochism which Mario Praz, in his brilliant work *The Romantic Agony*, has revealed as central to much Romantic writing.

Such then, along with Gray's conception of the poet in general, were some of the forces at work behind his writing of *The Bard*. His own period of actual translation had probably not yet begun, but his range of erudition was amazing. There was a two-year interval between his beginning and completing the ode, an interval in which his inspiration ran dry. He was stimulated into finishing the poem when John Parry, the blind Welsh harper, came to Cambridge '& scratch'd out such ravishing blind Harmony, such tunes of a thousand year old with names enough to choke you, as have set all this learned body a'dancing'.[29]

The historical background to the poem is the now exploded myth that Edward I, in Gray's words, 'is said to have hanged up all [the Welsh] Bards, because they encouraged the nation to rebellion, but their works (we see), still remain, the Language (tho' decaying) still lives, and the art of their versification is known, and practised to this day among them'.[30] The poem is thus a restatement of the idea that the artist is killed by tyranny, though the spirit of freedom he fosters lives on. This is the meaning of the Bard's prophecy. Gray preferred this poem to *The Progress of Poesy*, and it is easy to see why: the ideas are expressed concisely, though with a mass of esoteric detail, and in one magnificently dramatic gesture. The Bard, addressing Edward, details the bloody fate of his line down to the time of Richard III – 'the bristled Boar'. Then, with the Tudors, who claimed Welsh descent, and particularly with Elizabeth, Wales will again become the originator of liberty and art. Spenser, Shakespeare, and later Milton are to flourish, the Bard declares. He consigns Edward to despair, while defiantly confident of the future of his own race:

> . . . headlong from the mountain's height
> Deep in the roaring tide he plunged to endless night.

[29] *Corr.* 501–3.
[30] Gray's article *Cambri* in his Commonplace Book. Quoted Lonsdale.

The Bard is a magnificent poem, notable for vivid language and imagery which are all the more powerful for the rigid Pindaric form. If we compare the description of the Bard himself to the diction of, say, the *Ode on the Spring*, we can see how wide Gray's range is and in how small a number of poems it is achieved. This description is far removed from pastoral Rococo:

> On a rock, whose haughty brow
> Frowns o'er old Conway's foaming flood,
> Robed in the sable garb of woe,
> With haggard eyes the poet stood;
> (Loose his beard and hoary hair
> Streamed, like a meteor, to the troubled air)
> And, with a master's hand and prophet's fire,
> Struck the deep sorrows of his lyre.

This presentation of so striking a picture and incident is one of Gray's finest feats.

The publication of the Odes by Walpole in 1757 marks virtually the end of Gray's creative career. In the same year he declined the Laureateship. In 1768 his collected poems appeared and he was appointed Regius Professor of Modern History at Cambridge. Gray died on 30 July 1771 and was buried beside his mother in the churchyard at Stoke Poges, the traditional scene of the *Elegy*. A lonely, passionate scholar, he had written a handful of poems which stand beside the greatest in the language.

SELECT BIBLIOGRAPHY

EDITION

The Poems of Gray, Collins, and Goldsmith, edited by Roger Lonsdale, Longmans, 1969

The Correspondance of Thomas Gray, edited by Paget Toynbee and Leonard Whibley, 3 vols, Oxford, 1935

BIOGRAPHY

Thomas Gray: A Biography, R. W. Ketton-Cremer, Cambridge, 1955

CRITICISM

Matthew Arnold, 'Thomas Gray' in *Essays in Criticism* (2nd series)

Walter J. Bate, *From Classic to Romantic*, Harvard, 1946

Cleanth Brooks, *The Well Wrought Urn*, New York, 1947

William Empson, *Some Versions of Pastoral*, Chatto and Windus, 1935

Samuel Johnson, *Lives of the English Poets*, edited by G. B. Hill, O.U.P., 1905

Roger Martin, *Essai sur Thomas Gray*, O.U.P., 1935

A. L. Reed, *The Background of Gray's Elegy*, Russel and Russel Inc., New York, 1962

E. D. Snyder, *The Celtic Revival in English Literature*, Gloucester, Mass., 1965

NOTE ON THIS EDITION

This edition contains all Gray's authenticated English poems with the exception of the translations other than those from the Norse. The text is that of *The Poems of Thomas Gray, William Collins, Oliver Goldsmith*, edited by Roger Lonsdale for permission to use which I am indebted to the publisher Messrs Longman.

The portrait of Gray is that by Benjamin Wilson, in the possession of John Murray, to whom my thanks are due for permission to reproduce it.

I wish to express my gratitude to Stephen Coote of Magdalene College, Cambridge, for extensive help throughout the preparation of this volume.

J. R.

Lewes 1972

Lines Spoken by the Ghost of John Dennis at the Devil Tavern

From purling streams and the Elysian scene,
From groves that smile with never-fading green,
I reascend: in Atropos' despite
Restored to Celadon and upper light.
Ye gods, that sway the regions under ground,   5
Reveal to mortal view your realms profound;
At his command admit the eye of day:
When Celadon commands, what god can disobey?
Nor seeks he your Tartarean fires to know,
The house of torture and the abyss of woe;   10
But happy fields and mansions free from pain,
Gay meads and springing flowers, best please the
    gentle swain.
   That little, naked, melancholy thing,
My soul, when first she tried her flight to wing,
Began with speed new regions to explore,   15
And blundered through a narrow postern door.
First most devoutly having said its prayers,
It tumbled down a thousand pair of stairs,
Through entries long, through cellars vast and deep,
Where ghostly rats their habitations keep,   20
Where spiders spread their webs and owlish goblins
    sleep.
After so many chances had befell,
It came into a mead of asphodel:

Betwixt the confines of the light and dark
It lies, of 'Lysium the St. James's Park.   25
Here spirit-beaux flutter along the Mall,
And shadows in disguise skate o'er the iced Canal;
Here groves embowered and more sequestered shades,
Frequented by the ghosts of ancient maids,
Are seen to rise. The melancholy scene,   30
With gloomy haunts and twilight walks between,
Conceals the wayward band: here spend their time
Greensickness girls that died in youthful prime,
Virgins forlorn, all dressed in willow-green-i,
With Queen Elizabeth and Nicolini.   35

   More to reveal, or many words to use,
Would tire alike your patience and my muse.
Believe that never was so faithful found
Queen Proserpine to Pluto under ground,
Or Cleopatra to her Mark Antony,   40
As Orozmades to his Celadony.

   P.S. Lucrece for half a crown will show you fun,
But Mrs. Oldfield is become a nun.
Nobles and cits, Prince Pluto and his spouse,
Flock to the ghost of Covent-Garden House: 45
Plays, which were hissed above, below revive,
When dead applauded that were damned alive.
The people, as in life, still keep their passions,
But differ something from the world in fashions.
Queen Artemisia breakfasts on bohea,   50
And Alexander wears a ramilie.

Lines on Beech Trees

And, as they bow their hoary tops, relate
In murmuring sounds the dark decrees of fate;

While visions, as poetic eyes avow,
Cling to each leaf and swarm on every bough.

Agrippina, a Tragedy

DRAMATIS PERSONAE

Agrippina   *The Empress mother.*
Nero   *The Emperor.*
Poppaea   *Believed to be in love with Otho.*
Otho   *A young man of quality, in love with Poppaea.*
Seneca   *The Emperor's preceptor.*
Anicetus   *Captain of the the Guards.*
Demetrius   *The Cynic, friend to Seneca.*
Aceronia   *Confidante to Agrippina.*

Scene, the Emperor's villa at Baiae

THE ARGUMENT

The drama opens with the indignation of Agrippina, at receiving her son's orders from Anicetus to remove from Baiae, and to have her guard taken from her. At this time Otho having conveyed Poppaea from the house of her husband Rufus Crispinus, brings her to Baiae, where he means to conceal her among the croud; or, if his fraud is discovered, to have recourse to the Emperor's authority; but, knowing the lawless temper of Nero, he determines not to have recourse to that expedient, but on the utmost necessity. In the meantime he commits her to the care of Anicetus, whom he takes to be his friend, and in whose age he thinks he may safely confide. Nero is not yet come to Baiae: but Seneca, whom he sends before him, informs Agrippina of the accusation concerning Rubellius

Plancus, and desires her to clear herself, which she does briefly; but demands to see her son, who, on his arrival, acquits her of all suspicion, and restores her to her honours. In the meanwhile Anicetus, to whose care Poppaea had been entrusted by Otho, contrives the following plot to ruin Agrippina: He betrays his trust to Otho, and brings Nero, as it were by chance, to the sight of the beautiful Poppaea; the Emperor is immediately struck with her charms, and she, by a feigned resistance, increases his passion; tho', in reality, she is from the first dazzled with the prospect of empire, and forgets Otho: She therefore joins with Anicetus in his design of ruining Agrippina, soon perceiving that it will be for her interest. Otho hearing that the Emperor had seen Poppaea, is much enraged; but not knowing that this interview was obtained thro' the treachery of Anicetus, is readily persuaded by him to see Agrippina in secret, and acquaint her with his fears that her son Nero would marry Poppaea. Agrippina, to support her own power, and to wean the Emperor from the love of Poppaea, gives Otho encouragement, and promises to support him. Anicetus secretly introduces Nero to hear their discourse; who resolves immediately on his mother's death, and, by Anicetus's means, to destroy her by drowning. A solemn feast, in honour of their reconciliation, is to be made; after which she being to go by sea to Bauli, the ship is so contrived as to sink or crush her; she escapes by accident, and returns to Baiae. In this interval Otho has an interview with Poppaea; and being duped a second time by Anicetus and her, determines to fly with her into Greece, by means of a vessel whish is to be furnished by Anicetus; but he, pretending to remove Poppaea on board in the night, conveys her to Nero's apartment: She there encourages and determines Nero to banish Otho, and finish the horrid deed he had attempted on his mother. Anicetus undertakes to execute his resolves; and, under pretence of a plot upon the Emperor's life, is sent with a guard to murder Agrippina, who is still at Baiae in imminent fear, and irresolute how to conduct herself. The account of her death, and the Emperor's honour and fruitless remorse, finishes the drama.

ACT I.

[Agrippina.   Aceronia]

AGRIPPINA

'Tis well, begone! your errand is performed.

  [*Speaks as to* Anicetus *entering.*]

The message needs no comment. Tell your master,
His mother shall obey him. Say you saw her
Yielding due reverence to his high command:
Alone, unguarded and without a lictor   5
As fits the daughter of Germanicus.
Say, she retired to Antium; there to tend
Her household cares, a woman's best employment.
What if you add, how she turned pale and trembled:
You think, you spied a tear stand in her eye,   10
And would have dropped, but that her pride
      restrained it?
(Go! you can paint it well) 'twill profit you,
And please the stripling. Yet 'twould dash his joy
To hear the spirit of Britannicus
Yet walks on earth: at least there are who know   15
Without a spell to raise, and bid it fire
A thousand haughty hearts, unused to shake
When a boy frowns, nor to be lured with smiles
To taste of hollow kindness, or partake
His hospitable board: they are aware   20
Of the unpledged bowl, they love not aconite.

ACERONIA

He's gone; and much I hope these walls alone
And the mute air are privy to your passion.
Forgive your servant's fears, who sees the danger

Which fierce resentment cannot fail to raise   25
In haughty youth and irritated power.

AGRIPPINA

And dost thou talk to me, to me, of danger,
Of haughty youth and irritated power,
To her that gave it being, her that armed
This painted Jove, and taught his novice hand   30
To aim the forked bolt; while he stood trembling,
Scared at the sound and dazzled with its brightness?
   'Tis like, thou hast forgot, when yet a stranger
To adoration, to the grateful steam
Of flattery's incense and obsequious vows   35
From voluntary realms, a puny boy,
Decked with no other lustre than the blood
Of Agrippina's race, he lived unknown
To fame or fortune; haply eyed at distance
Some edileship, ambitious of the power   40
To judge of weights and measures; scarcely dared
On expectation's strongest wing to soar
High as the consulate, that empty shade
Of long-forgotten liberty: when I
Oped his young eye to bear the blaze of greatness;   45
Showed him where empire towered, and bade him
      strike
The noble quarry. Gods! then was the time
To shrink from danger; fear might then have worn
The mask of prudence; but a heart like mine,
A heart that glows with the pure Julian fire,   50
If bright ambition from her craggy seat
Display the radiant prize, will mount undaunted,
Gain the rough heights, and grasp the dangerous
      honour.

ACERONIA

Through various life I have pursued your steps,
Have seen your soul, and wondered at its daring: 55

Hence rise my fears. Nor am I yet to learn
How vast the debt of gratitude which Nero
To such a mother owes; the world you gave him
Suffices not to pay the obligation.
   I well remember too (for I was present)   60
When in a secret and dead hour of night,
Due sacrifice performed with barbarous rites
Of muttered charms and solemn invocation,
You bade the Magi call the dreadful powers
That read futurity, to know the fate   65
Impending o'er your son: their answer was,
If the son reign, the mother perishes.
Perish (you cried) the mother! reign the son!
He reigns, the rest is heaven's; who oft has bade,
Even when its will seemed wrote in lines of blood,   70
The unthought event disclose a whiter meaning.
Think too how oft in weak and sickly minds
The sweets of kindness lavishly indulged
Rankle to gall; and benefits too great
To be repaid, sit heavy on the soul,   75
As unrequited wrongs. The willing homage
Of prostrate Rome, the senate's joint applause,
The riches of the earth, the train of pleasures
That wait on youth and arbitrary sway:
These were your gift, and with them you bestowed   80
The very power he has to be ungrateful.

AGRIPPINA

Thus ever grave and undisturbed reflection
Pours its cool dictates in the madding ear
Of rage, and thinks to quench the fire it feels not.
Sayest thou I must be cautious, must be silent,   85
And tremble at the phantom I have raised?
Carry to him they timid counsels. He
Perchance may heed 'em: tell him too, that one
Who had such liberal power to give, may still

With equal power resume that gift, and raise   90
A tempest that shall shake her own creation
To its original atoms—tell me! say,
This mighty emperor, this dreaded hero,
Has he beheld the glittering front of war?
Knows his soft ear the trumpet's thrilling voice,   95
And outcry of the battle? Have his limbs
Sweat under iron harness? Is he not
The silken son of dalliance, nursed in ease
And pleasure's flowery lap? Rubellius lives,
And Sylla has his friends, though schooled by fear   100
To bow the supple knee, and court the times
With shows of fair obeisance; and a call
Like mine might serve belike to wake pretensions
Drowsier than theirs, who boast the genuine blood
Of our imperial house. [Cannot my nod]   105
Rouse [up] eight hardy legions, wont to stem
With stubborn nerves the tide, and face the rigour
Of bleak Germania's snows [?] Four, not less brave,
That in Armenia quell the Parthian force
Under the warlike Corbulo, by [me]   110
Marked for their leader: these, by ties confirmed
Of old respect and gratitude, are [mine].
Surely the Masians too, and those of Egypt,
Have not forgot [my] sire: the eye of Rome
And the Praetorian camp have long revered,   115
With customed awe, the daughter, sister, wife,
And mother of their Caesars. Ha! by Juno,
It bears a noble semblance. On this base
My great revenge shall rise; or say we sound
The trump of liberty; there will not want,   120
Even in the servile senate, ears to own
Her spirit-stirring voice; Soranus there,
And Cassius; Veto too, and Thrasea,
Minds of the antique cast, rough, stubborn souls,

44

That struggle with the yoke. How shall the spark   125
Unquenchable, that glows within their breasts,
Blaze into freedom, when the idle herd
(Slaves from the womb, created but to stare
And bellow in the Circus) yet will start,
And shake 'em at the name of liberty,   130
Stung by a senseless word, a vain tradition,
As there were magic in it? Wrinkled beldams
Teach it their grandchildren, as somewhat rare
That anciently appeared, but when, extends
Beyond their chronicle—oh! 'tis a cause   135
To arm the hand of childhood, and rebrace
The slackened sinews of time-wearied age.
    Yes, we may meet, ungrateful boy, we may!
Again the buried Genius of old Rome
Shall from the dust uprear his reverend head,   140
Roused by the shout of millions: there before
His high tribunal thou and I appear.
Let majesty sit on thy awful brow
And lighten from thy eye: around thee call
The gilded swarm that wantons in the sunshine   145
Of thy full favour; Seneca be there
In gorgeous phrase of laboured eloquence
To dress thy plea, and Burrhus strengthen it
With his plain soldier's oath and honest seeming.
Against thee, liberty and Agrippina: 150
The world, the prize; and fair befall the victors.
    But soft! why do I waste the fruitless hours
In threats unexecuted? Haste thee, fly
These hated walls that seem to mock my shame,
And cast me forth in duty to their lord.   155
    My thought aches at him; not the basilisk
More deadly to the sight than is to me
The cool injurious eye of frozen kindness.
I will not meet its poison. Let him feel

Before he sees me. Yes, I will be gone, 160
But not to Antium—all shall be confessed,
Whate'er the frivolous tongue of giddy fame
Has spread among the crowd; things that but
    whispered
Have arched the hearer's brow and riveted
His eyes in fearful ecstasy: no matter 165
What, so it be strange, and dreadful—sorceries,
Assassinations, poisonings; the deeper
My guilt, the blacker his ingratitude.
   And you, ye manes of ambition's victims,
Enshrined Claudius, with the pitied ghosts 170
Of the Syllani, doomed to early death
(Ye unavailing horrors, fruitless crimes!),
If from the realms of night my voice ye hear,
In lieu of penitence and vain remorse,
Accept my vengeance. Though by me ye bled, 175
He was the cause. My love, my fears for him,
Dried the soft springs of pity in my heart,
And froze them up with deadly cruelty.
Yet if your injured shades demand my fate,
If murder cries for murder, blood for blood, 180
Let me not fall alone; but crush his pride,
And sink the traitor in his mother's ruin. [*Exeunt.*]

SCENE II.
[Otho, Poppaea]

OTHO

Thus far we're safe. Thanks to the rosy queen
Of amorous thefts: and had her wanton son
Lent us his wings, we could not have beguiled 185
With more elusive speed the dazzled sight
Of wakeful jealousy. Be gay securely;

Dispel, my fair, with smiles, the timorous cloud
That hangs on thy clear brow. So Helen looked,
So her white neck reclined, so was she borne   190
By the young Trojan to his gilded bark
With fond reluctance, yielding modesty,
And oft reverted eye, as if she knew not
Whether she feared or wished to be pursued.

Ode on the Spring

Lo! where the rosy-bosomed Hours,
Fair Venus' train, appear,
Disclose the long-expecting flowers,
And wake the purple year!
The Attic warbler pours her throat,   5
Responsive to the cuckoo's note,
The untaught harmony of spring:
While whispering pleasure as they fly,
Cool zephyrs through the clear blue sky
Their gathered fragrance fling.   10
Where'er the oak's thick branches stretch
A broader browner shade;
Where'er the rude and moss-grown beech
O'er-canopies the glade,
Beside some water's rushy brink   15
With me the Muse shall sit, and think
(At ease reclined in rustic state)
How vain the ardour of the crowd,
How low, how little are the proud,
How indigent the great!   20

Still is the toiling hand of Care;
The panting herds repose.

Yet hark, how through the peopled air
The busy murmur glows!
The insect youth are on the wing,   25
Eager to taste the honeyed spring,
And float amid the liquid noon:
Some lightly o'er the current skim,
Some show their gaily-gilded trim
Quick-glancing to the sun.   30

To Contemplation's sober eye
Such is the race of man:
And they that creep, and they that fly,
Shall end where they began.
Alike the busy and the gay   35
But flutter through life's little day,
In fortune's varying colours dressed:
Brushed by the hand of rough Mischance,
Or chilled by age, their airy dance
They leave, in dust to rest.   40

Methinks I hear in accents low
The sportive kind reply:
Poor moralist! and what art thou?
A solitary fly!
Thy joys no glittering female meets,   45
No hive hast thou of hoarded sweets,
No painted plumage to display:
On hasty wings thy youth is flown;
Thy sun is set, thy spring is gone————
We frolic, while 'tis May.   50

Ode on a Distant Prospect of Eton College

"Άνθρωπος· ἱκανὴ πρόφασις εἰς τὸ δυστυχεῖν.

Ye distant spires, ye antique towers,
That crown the watery glade,
Where grateful Science still adores
Her Henry's holy shade;
And ye that from the stately brow   5
Of Windsor's heights the expanse below
Of grove, of lawn, of mead survey,
Whose turf, whose shade, whose flowers among
Wanders the hoary Thames along
His silver-winding way.   10

Ah, happy hills, ah, pleasing shade,
Ah, fields beloved in vain,
Where once my careless childhood strayed,
A stranger yet to pain!
I feel the gales, that from ye blow,   15
A momentary bliss bestow,
As waving fresh their gladsome wing,
My weary soul they seem to soothe,
And, redolent of joy and youth,
To breathe a second spring.   20

Say, Father Thames, for thou hast seen
Full many a sprightly race
Disporting on thy margent green
The paths of pleasure trace,
Who foremost now delight to cleave   25
With pliant arm thy glassy wave?

49

The captive linnet which enthrall?
What idle progeny succeed
To chase the rolling circle's speed,
Or urge the flying ball?   30

    While some on earnest business bent
Their murmuring labours ply
'Gainst graver hours, that bring constraint
To sweeten liberty:
Some bold adventurers disdain   35
The limits of their little reign,
And unknown regions dare descry:
Still as they run they look behind,
They hear a voice in every wind,
And snatch a fearful joy.   40

    Gay hope is theirs by fancy fed,
Less pleasing when possessed;
The tear forgot as soon as shed,
The sunshine of the breast:
Theirs buxom health of rosy hue,   45
Wild wit, invention ever-new,
And lively cheer of vigour born;
The thoughtless day, the easy night,
The spirits pure, the slumbers light,
That fly the approach of morn.   50

    Alas, regardless of their doom,
The little victims play!
No sense have they of ills to come,
Nor care beyond today:
Yet see how all around 'em wait   55
The ministers of human fate,
And black Misfortune's baleful train!
Ah, show them where in ambush stand

To seize their prey the murtherous band!
Ah, tell them, they are men!   60

These shall the fury Passions tear,
The vultures of the mind,
Disdainful Anger, pallid Fear,
And Shame that skulks behind;
Or pining Love shall waste their youth,   65
Or jealousy with rankling tooth,
That inly gnaws the secret heart,
And Envy wan, and faded Care,
Grim-visaged comfortless Despair,
And Sorrow's piercing dart.   70

Ambition this shall tempt to rise,
Then whirl the wretch from high,
To bitter Scorn a sacrifice,
And grinning Infamy.
The stings of Falsehood those shall try,   75
And hard Unkindness' altered eye,
That mocks the tear it forced to flow;
And keen Remorse with blood defiled,
And moody Madness laughing wild
Amid severest woe.   80

Lo, in the vale of years beneath
A grisly troop are seen,
The painful family of Death,
More hideous than their Queen:
This racks the joints, this fires the veins,   85
That every labouring sinew strains,
Those in the deeper vitals rage:
Lo, Poverty, to fill the band,
That numbs the soul with icy hand,
And slow-consuming Age.   90

To each his sufferings: all are men,
Condemned alike to groan;
The tender for another's pain,
The unfeeling for his own.
Yet ah! why should they know their fate?   95
Since sorrow never comes too late,
And happiness too swiftly flies.
Thought would destroy their paradise.
No more; where ignorance is bliss,
'Tis folly to be wise.   100

Sonnet on the Death of Mr Richard West

In vain to me the smiling mornings shine,
And reddening Phoebus lifts his golden fire:
The birds in vain their amorous descant join,
Or cheerful fields resume their green attire:
These ears, alas! for other notes repine,   5
A different object do these eyes require.
My lonely anguish melts no heart but mine;
And in my breast the imperfect joys expire.
Yet morning smiles the busy race to cheer,
And new-born pleasure brings to happier men: 10
The fields to all their wonted tribute bear;
To warm their little loves the birds complain.
I fruitless mourn to him that cannot hear,
And weep the more because I weep in vain.

Ode to Adversity

Τοῦ φρονεῖν βροτοὺς ὁδώ-
σαντα, τῷ πάθει μάθαν
θέντα κυρίως ἔχειν.

Daughter of Jove, relentless power,
Thou tamer of the human breast,
Whose iron scourge and torturing hour,
The bad affright, afflict the best!
Bound in thy adamantine chain   5
The proud are taught to taste of pain,
And purple tyrants vainly groan
With pangs unfelt before, unpitied and alone.

When first thy Sire to send on earth
Virtue, his darling child, designed,   10
To thee he gave the heavenly birth,
And bade to form her infant mind.
Stern rugged nurse! thy rigid lore
With patience many a year she bore:
What sorrow was, thou bad'st her know,   15
And from her own she learned to melt at others' woe.

Scared at thy frown terrific, fly
Self-pleasing Folly's idle brood,
Wild Laughter, Noise, and thoughtless Joy,
And leave us leisure to be good.   20
Light they disperse, and with them go
The summer friend, the flattering foe;
By vain Prosperity received,
To her they vow their truth and are again believed.

Wisdom in sable garb arrayed,   25
Immersed in rapturous thought profound,
And Melancholy, silent maid
With leaden eye that loves the ground,
Still on thy solemn steps attend:
Warm Charity, the general friend,   30
With Justice to herself severe,
And Pity, dropping soft the sadly-pleasing tear.

Oh, gently on thy suppliant's head,
Dread goddess, lay thy chastening hand!
Not in thy Gorgon terrors clad,   35
Nor circled with the vengeful band
(As by the impious thou art seen)
With thundering voice and threatening mien,
With screaming Horror's funeral cry,
Despair and fell Disease and ghastly Poverty.   40

Thy form benign, oh Goddess, wear,
Thy milder influence impart,
Thy philosophic train be there
To soften, not to wound my heart.
The generous spark extinct revive,   45
Teach me to love and to forgive,
Exact my own defects to scan,
What others are to feel, and know myself a man.

Hymn to Ignorance
A Fragment

Hail, horrors, hail! ye ever-gloomy bowers,
Ye gothic fanes and antiquated towers,
Where rushy Camus' slowly-winding flood
Perpetual draws his humid train of mud:
Glad I revisit thy neglected reign;   5
Oh, take me to thy peaceful shade again.
   But chiefly thee, whose influence breathed from high
Augments the native darkness of the sky;
Ah, Ignorance! soft salutary power!
Prostrate with filial reverence I adore.   10
Thrice hath Hyperion rolled his annual race,
Since weeping I forsook thy fond embrace.
Oh say, successful dost thou still oppose
Thy leaden aegis 'gainst our ancient foes?
Still stretch, tenacious of thy right divine,   15
The massy sceptre o'er thy slumbering line?
And dews Lethean through the land dispense
To steep in slumbers each benighted sense?
If any spark of wit's delusive ray
Break out, and flash a momentary day,   20
With damp, cold touch forbid it to aspire,
And huddle up in fogs the dangerous fire.
   Oh say—she hears me not, but, careless grown,
Lethargic nods upon her ebon throne.
Goddess! awake, arise! alas, my fears!   25
Can powers immortal feel the force of years?
Not thus of old, with ensigns wide unfurled,
She rode triumphant o'er the vanquished world;

Fierce nations owned her unresisted might,
And all was Ignorance, and all was Night.   30
  Oh! sacred age! Oh! times for ever lost!
(The schoolman's glory, and the churchman's boast.)
For ever gone—yet still to Fancy new,
Her rapid wings the transient scene pursue.
And bring the buried ages back to view.   35
  High on her car, behold the grandam ride
Like old Sesostris with barbaric pride;
. . . a team of harnessed monarchs bend . . ..

Ode on the Death of a Favourite Cat, Drowned in a Tub of Gold Fishes

'Twas on a lofty vase's side,
Where China's gayest art had dyed
  The azure flowers, that blow;
Demurest of the tabby kind,
The pensive Selima reclined,   5
  Gazed on the lake below.

Her conscious tail her joy declared;
The fair round face, the snowy beard,
  The velvet of her paws,
Her coat that with the tortoise vies,   10
Her ears of jet and emerald eyes,
  She saw; and purred applause.

Still had she gazed; but 'midst the tide
Two angel forms were seen to glide,
  The genii of the stream: 15
Their scaly armour's Tyrian hue

Through richest purple to the view
    Betrayed a golden gleam.

The hapless nymph with wonder saw:
A whisker first and then a claw,   20
    With many an ardent wish,
She stretched in vain to reach the prize.
What female heart can gold despise?
    What cat's averse to fish?

Presumptuous maid! with looks intent   25
Again stretched, again she bent,
    Nor knew the gulf between.
(Malignant Fate sat by and smiled)
The slippery verge her feet beguiled,
    She tumbled headlong in.   30

Eight times emerging from the flood
She mewed to every watery god,
    Some speedy aid to send.
No dolphin came, no Nereid stirred:
Nor cruel Tom nor Susan heard.   35
    A favourite has no friend!

From hence, ye beauties, undeceived,
Know, one false step is ne'er retrieved,
    And be with caution bold.
Not all that tempts your wandering eyes   40
And heedless hearts is lawful prize;
    Nor all that glisters gold.

The Alliance of Education and Government
A Fragment

ESSAY I

. . . πόταγ', ὦ 'γαθέ· τὰν γὰρ ἀοιδάν
οὔτι πα εἰς 'Αΐδαν γε τὸν ἐκλελάθοντα φυλαξεῖς.
                                    THEOC[RITUS].

As sickly plants betray a niggard earth,
Whose barren bosom starves her generous birth,
Nor genial warmth nor genial juice retains
Their roots to feed and fill their verdant veins;
And as in climes, where winter holds his reign,   5
The soil, though fertile, will not teem in vain,
Forbids her gems to swell, her shades to rise,
Nor trusts her blossoms to the churlish skies:
So draw mankind in vain the vital airs,
Unformed, unfriended, by those kindly cares   10
That health and vigour to the soul impart,
Spread the young thought and warm the opening heart.
So fond Instruction on the growing powers
Of nature idly lavishes her stores,
If equal justice with unclouded face   15
Smile not indulgent on the rising race,
And scatter with a free though frugal hand
Light golden showers of plenty o'er the land:
But Tyranny has fixed her empire there,   ⎫
To check their tender hopes with chilling fear,   ⎬   20
And blast the blooming promise of the year.   ⎭
  This spacious animated scene survey

From where the rolling orb, that gives the day,
His sable sons with nearer course surrounds,
To either pole and life's remotest bounds. 25
How rude so e'er the exterior form we find,
Howe'er opinion tinge the varied mind,
Alike to all the kind impartial heaven
The sparks of truth and happiness has given:
With sense to feel, with memory to retain, 30
They follow pleasure and they fly from pain;
Their judgement mends the plan their fancy draws,
The event presages and explores the cause.
The soft returns of gratitude they know,
By fraud elude, by force repel the foe; 35
While mutual wishes, mutual woes, endear
The social smile and sympathetic tear.
　　Say then, through ages by what fate confined
To different climes seem different souls assigned?
Here measured laws and philosophic ease 40
Fix and improve the polished arts of peace.
There Industry and Gain their vigils keep,
Command the winds and tame the unwilling deep.
Here force and hardy deeds of blood prevail;
There languid pleasure sighs in every gale. 45
Oft o'er the trembling nations from afar
Has Scythia breathed the living cloud of war;
And, where the deluge burst, with sweepy sway
Their arms, their kings, their gods were rolled away.
As oft have issued, host impelling host, 50
The blue-eyed myriads from the Baltic coast.
The prostrate south to the destroyer yields
Her boasted titles and her golden fields:
With grim delight the brood of winter view
A brighter day and heavens of azure hue, 55
Scent the new fragrance of the breathing rose,
And quaff the pendent vintage, as it grows.

Proud of the yoke and pliant to the rod,
Why yet does Asia dread a monarch's nod,
While European freedom still withstands   60
The encroaching tide, that drowns her lessening lands,
And sees far off with an indignant groan
Her native plains and empires once her own?
Can opener skies and suns of fiercer flame
O'erpower the fire that animates our frame,   65
As lamps, that shed at even a cheerful ray,
Fade and expire beneath the eye of day?
Need we the influence of the northern star
To string our nerves and steel our hearts to war?
And, where the face of nature laughs around,   70
Must sickening Virtue fly the tainted ground?
Unmanly thought! what seasons can control,
What fancied zone can circumscribe the Soul,
Who, conscious of the source from whence she springs,
By Reason's light on Resolution's wings,   75
Spite of her frail companion, dauntless goes
O'er Libya deserts and through Zembla's snows?
She bids each slumbering energy awake,
Another touch, another temper take,
Suspends the inferior laws that rule our clay: 80
The stubborn elements confess her sway;
Their little wants, their low desires, refine,
And raise the mortal to a height divine.
    Not but the human fabric from the birth
Imbibes a flavour of its parent earth: 85
As various tracts enforce a various toil,
The manners speak the idiom of their toil,
An iron-race the mountain-cliffs maintain,
Foes to the gentler genius of the plain:
For where unwearied sinews must be found   90
With sidelong plough to quell the flinty ground,
To turn the torrent's swift-descending flood,

To brave the savage rushing from the wood,
What wonder if, to patient valour trained,
They guard with spirit what by strength they gained;   95
And while their rocky ramparts round they see,
The rough abode of want and liberty,
(As lawless force from confidence will grow)
Insult the plenty of the vales below?
What wonder in the sultry climes, that spread   100
Where Nile redundant o'er his summer-bed
From his broad bosom life and verdure flings,
And broods o'er Egypt with his watery wings,
If with adventurous oar and ready sail,
The dusky people drive before the gale,   105
Or on frail floats to distant cities ride,
That rise and glitter o'er the ambient tide.

Tophet

Such Tophet was; so looked the grinning fiend
Whom many a frighted prelate called his friend;
I saw them bow and, while they wished him dead,
With servile simper nod the mitred head.
Our Mother-Church with half-averted sight   5
Blushed as she blessed her grisly proselyte:
Hosannahs rung through Hell's tremendous borders,
And Satan's self had thoughts of taking orders.

Elegy Written in a Country Churchyard

The curfew tolls the knell of parting day,
The lowing herd wind slowly o'er the lea,

The ploughman homeward plods his weary way,
And leaves the world to darkness and to me.

Now fades the glimmering landscape on the sight,   5
And all the air a solemn stillness holds,
Save where the beetle wheels his droning flight,
And drowsy tinklings lull the distant folds;

Save that from yonder ivy-mantled tower
The moping owl does to the moon complain   10
Of such as, wandering near her secret bower,
Molest her ancient solitary reign.

Beneath those rugged elms, that yew-tree's shade,
Where heaves the turf in many a mouldering heap,
Each in his narrow cell for ever laid,   15
The rude forefathers of the hamlet sleep.

The breezy call of incense-breathing morn,
The swallow twittering from the straw-built shed,
The cock's shrill clarion or the echoing horn,
No more shall rouse them from their lowly bed.   20

For them no more the blazing hearth shall burn,
Or busy housewife ply her evening care:
No children run to lisp their sire's return,
Or climb his knees the envied kiss to share.

Oft did the harvest to their sickle yield,   25
Their furrow oft the stubborn glebe has broke;
How jocund did they drive their team afield!
How bowed the woods beneath their sturdy stroke!

Let not Ambition mock their useful toil,
Their homely joys and destiny obscure;   30

Nor Grandeur hear, with a disdainful smile,
The short and simple annals of the poor.

The boast of heraldry, the pomp of power,
And all that beauty, all that wealth e'er gave,
Awaits alike the inevitable hour.   35
The paths of glory lead but to the grave.

Nor you, ye Proud, impute to these the fault,
If Memory o'er their tomb no trophies raise,
Where through the long-drawn aisle and fretted vault
The pealing anthem swells the note of praise.   40

Can storied urn or animated bust
Back to its mansion call the fleeting breath?
Can Honour's voice provoke the silent dust,
Or Flattery soothe the dull cold ear of Death?

Perhaps in this neglected spot is laid   45
Some heart once pregnant with celestial fire;
Hands that the rod of empire might have swayed,
Or waked to ecstasy the living lyre.

But Knowledge to their eyes her ample page
Rich with the spoils of time did ne'er unroll;   50
Chill Penury repressed their noble rage,
And froze the genial current of the soul.

Full many a gem of purest ray serene
The dark unfathomed caves of ocean bear:
Full many a flower is born to blush unseen   55
And waste its sweetness on the desert air.

Some village-Hampden that with dauntless breast
The little tyrant of his fields withstood;

Some mute inglorious Milton here may rest,
Some Cromwell guiltless of his country's blood.   60

The applause of listening senates to command,
The threats of pain and ruin to despise,
To scatter plenty o'er a smiling land,
And read their history in a nation's eyes,

Their lot forbade: nor circumscribed alone   65
Their growing virtues, but their crimes confined;
Forbade to wade through slaughter to a throne,
And shut the gates of mercy on mankind,

The struggling pangs of conscious truth to hide,
To quench the blushes of ingenuous shame,   70
Or heap the shrine of Luxury and Pride
With incense kindled at the Muse's flame.

Far from the madding crowd's ignoble strife
Their sober wishes never learned to stray;
Along the cool sequestered vale of life   75
They kept the noiseless tenor of their way.

Yet even these bones from insult to protect
Some frail memorial still erected nigh,
With uncouth rhymes and shapeless sculpture decked,
Implore the passing tribute of a sigh.   80

Their name, their years, spelt by the unlettered muse,
The place of fame and elegy supply:
And many a holy text around she strews,
That teach the rustic moralist to die.

For who to dumb Forgetfulness a prey,   85
This pleasing anxious being e'er resigned,

Left the warm precincts of the cheerful day,
Nor cast one longing lingering look behind?

On some fond breast the parting soul relies,
Some pious drops the closing eye requires;   90
Ev'n from the tomb the voice of nature cries,
Ev'n in our ashes live their wonted fires.

For thee who, mindful of the unhonoured dead,
Dost in these lines their artless tale relate;
If chance, by lonely Contemplation led,   95
Some kindred spirit shall inquire thy fate,

Haply some hoary-headed swain may say,
'Oft have we seen him at the peep of dawn
'Brushing with hasty steps the dews away
'To meet the sun upon the upland lawn.   100

'There at the foot of yonder nodding beech
'That wreathes its old fantastic roots so high,
'His listless length at noontide would he stretch,
'And pore upon the brook that babbles by.

'Hard by yon wood, now smiling as in scorn,   105
'Muttering his wayward fancies he would rove,
'Now drooping, woeful wan, like one forlorn,
'Or crazed with care, or crossed in hopeless love.

'One morn I missed him on the customed hill,
'Along the heath and near his favourite tree;   110
'Another came; nor yet beside the rill,
'Nor up the lawn, nor at the wood was he;

'The next with dirges due in sad array
'Slow through the church-way path we saw him borne.

'Approach and read (for thou can'st read) the lay,   115
'Graved on the stone beneath yon aged thorn.'

Here rests his head upon the lap of earth
A youth to fortune and to fame unknown.
Fair Science frowned not on his humble birth,
And Melancholy marked him for her own.   120

Large was his bounty and his soul sincere,
Heaven did a recompence as largely send:
He gave to Misery all he had, a tear,
He gained from Heaven ('twas all he wished) a friend.

No farther seek his merits to disclose,   125
Or draw his frailties from their dread abode.
(There they alike in trembling hope repose)
The bosom of his Father and his God.

A Long Story

In Britain's isle, no matter where,
An ancient pile of building stands:
The Huntingdons and Hattons there
Employed the power of fairy hands

To raise the ceiling's fretted height,   5
Each panel in achievements clothing,
Rich windows that exclude the light,
And passages that lead to nothing.

Full oft within the spacious walls,
When he had fifty winters o'er him,   10
My grave Lord-Keeper led the brawls;
The Seal and Maces danced before him.

His bushy beard and shoe-strings green,
His high-crowned hat and satin-doublet,
Moved the stout heart of England's Queen,   15
Though Pope and Spaniard could not trouble it.

What, in the very first beginning!
Shame of the versifying tribe!
Your history whither are you spinning?
Can you do nothing but describe?   20

A house there is (and that's enough)
From whence one fatal morning issues
A brace of warriors, not in buff,
But rustling in their silks and tissues.

The first came cap-a-pee from France   25
Her conquering destiny fulfilling,
Whom meaner beauties eye askance,
And vainly ape her art of killing.

The other Amazon kind heaven
Had armed with spirit, wit, and satire: 30
But Cobham had the polish given,
And tipped her arrows with good-nature.

To celebrate her eyes, her air——
Coarse panegyrics would but tease her.
Melissa is her nom de guerre.   35
Alas, who would not wish to please her!

With bonnet blue and capucine,
And aprons long they hid their armour,
And veiled their weapons bright and keen
In pity to the country-farmer.   40

Fame in the shape of Mr. P——t
(By this time all the parish know it)
Had told that thereabouts there lurked
A wicked imp they call a poet,

Who prowled the country far and near,   45
Bewitched the children of the peasants,
Dried up the cows and lamed the deer,
And sucked the eggs and killed the pheasants.

My lady heard their joint petition,
Swore by her coronet and ermine,   50
She'd issue out her high commission
To rid the manor of such vermin.

The heroines undertook the task;
Through lanes unknown, o'er stiles they ventured,
Rapped at the door nor stayed to ask,   55
But bounce into the parlour entered.

The trembling family they daunt,
They flirt, they sing, they laugh, they tattle,
Rummage his mother, pinch his aunt,
And up stairs in a whirlwind rattle.   60

Each hole and cupboard they explore,
Each creek and cranny of his chamber,
Run hurry-skurry round the floor,
And o'er the bed and tester clamber,

Into the drawers and china pry,   65
Papers and books, a huge imbroglio!
Under a tea-cup he might lie,
Or creased, like dogs-ears, in a folio.

On the first marching of the troops
The Muses, hopeless of his pardon,   70
Conveyed him underneath their hoops
To a small closet in the garden.

So Rumour says (who will, believe)
But that they left the door ajar,
Where, safe and laughing in his sleeve,   75
He heard the distant din of war.

Short was his joy. He little knew
The power of magic was no fable.
Out of the window, whisk, they flew,
But left a spell upon the table.   80

The words too eager to unriddle,
The poet felt a strange disorder:
Transparent birdlime formed the middle,
And chains invisible the border.

So cunning was the apparatus,   85
The powerful pothooks did so move him,
That, will he, nill he, to the Great-House
He went, as if the Devil drove him.

Yet no his way (no sign of grace,
For folks in fear are apt to pray)   90
To Phoebus he preferred his case,
And begged his aid that dreadful day.

The godhead would have backed his quarrel,
But, with a blush on recollection,
Owned that his quiver and his laurel   95
'Gainst four such eyes were no protection.

The court was sate, the culprit there,
Forth from their gloomy mansions creeping
The Lady Janes and Joans repair,
And from the gallery stand peeping: 100

Such as in silence of the night
Come (sweep) along some winding entry
(Styack has often seen the sight)
Or at the chapel-door stand sentry;

In peaked hoods and mantles tarnished,   105
Sour visages, enough to scare ye,
High dames of honour once, that garnished
The drawing-room of fierce Queen Mary!

The peeress comes. The audience stare,
And doff their hats with due submission: 110
She curtsies, as she takes her chair,
To all the people of condition.

The bard with many an artful fib
Had in imagination fenced him,
Disproved the arguments of Squib,   115
And all that Groom could urge against him.

But soon his rhetoric forsook him,
When he the solemn hall had seen;
A sudden fit of ague shook him,
He stood as mute as poor Macleane.   120

Yet something he was heard to mutter,
'How in the park beneath an old-tree
'(Without design to hurt the butter,
'Or any malice to the poultry,)

'He once or twice had penned a sonnet;   125
'Yet hoped that he might save his bacon:
'Numbers would give their oaths upon it,
'He ne'er was for a conjurer taken.'

The ghostly prudes with hagged face
Already had condemned the sinner.   130
My lady rose and with a grace——
She smiled, and bid him come to dinner.

'Jesu-Maria! Madam Bridget,
'Why, what can the Viscountess mean?'
(Cried the square hoods in woeful fidget)   135
'The times are altered quite and clean!

'Decorum's turned to mere civility;
'Her air and all her manners show it.
'Commend me to her affability!
'Speak to a commoner and poet!'   140

(*Here 500 stanzas are lost.*)

And so God save our noble King,
And guard us from long-winded lubbers,
That to eternity would sing,
And keep my lady from her rubbers.

Stanzas to Mr Bentley

In silent gaze the tuneful choir among,
    Half pleased, half blushing, let the Muse admire,
While Bentley leads her sister-art along,
    And bids the pencil answer to the lyre.
See, in their course, each transitory thought   5
    Fixed by his touch a lasting essence take;
Each dream, in fancy's airy colouring wrought,
    To local symmetry and life awake!
The tardy rhymes that used to linger on,
    To censure cold and negligent of fame,   10
In swifter measures animated run,
    And catch a lustre from his genuine flame.
Ah! could they catch his strength, his easy grace,
    His quick creation, his unerring line;
The energy of Pope they might efface,   15
    And Dryden's harmony submit to mine.
But not to one in this benighted age
    Is that diviner inspiration given,
That burns in Shakespeare's or in Milton's page,
    The pomp and prodigality of heaven.   20
As when, conspiring in the diamond's blaze,
    The meaner gems, that singly charm the sight,
Together dart their intermingled rays,
    And dazzle with a luxury of light.
Enough for me, if to some feeling breast   25
    My lines a secret sympathy [   ]
And as their pleasing influence [   ]
    A sigh of soft reflection [   ].

The Progress of Poesy
A Pindaric Ode

φωνᾶντα συνετοῖσιν ·ἐς
δὲ τὸ πᾶν ἑρμηνέων χατίζει.

PINDAR, Olymp[ian Odes] II.

I. 1

Awake, Aeolian lyre, awake,
And give to rapture all thy trembling strings.
From Helicon's harmonious springs
A thousand rills their mazy progress take:
The laughing flowers, that round them blow,   5
Drink life and fragrance as they flow.
Now the rich stream of music winds along,
Deep, majestic, smooth, and strong,
Through verdant vales and Ceres' golden reign:
Now rolling down the steep amain,   10
Headlong, impetuous, see it pour:
The rocks and nodding groves rebellow to the roar.

I. 2

Oh! Sovereign of the willing soul,
Parent of sweet and solemn-breathing airs,
Enchanting shell! the sullen Cares   15
And frantic Passions hear thy soft control.
On Thracia's hills the Lord of War
Has curbed the fury of his car,
And dropped his thirsty lance at thy command.
Perching on the sceptered hand   20

73

Of Jove, thy magic lulls the feathered king
With ruffled plumes and flagging wing:
Quenched in dark clouds of slumber lie
The terror of his beak and lightnings of his eye.

I.   3

Thee the voice, the dance, obey,   25
Tempered to thy warbled lay.
O'er Idalia's velvet-green
The rosy-crowned Loves are seen
On Cythera's day
With antic Sports and blue-eyed Pleasures,   30
Frisking light in frolic measures;
Now pursuing, now retreating,
Now in circling troops they meet:
To brisk notes in cadence beating
Glance their many-twinkling feet.   35
Slow melting strains their queen's approach declare:
Where'er she turns the Graces homage pay.
With arms sublime, that float upon the air,
In gliding state she wins her easy way:
O'er her warm cheek and rising bosom move   40
The bloom of young desire and purple light of love.

II.   I

Man's feeble race what ills await,
Labour, and penury, the racks of pain,
Disease, and sorrow's weeping train,
And death, sad refuge from the storms of fate!   45
The fond complaint, my song, disprove,
And justify the laws of Jove.
Say, has he given in vain the heavenly Muse?
Night and all her sickly dews,
Her spectres wan and birds of boding cry,   50

74

He gives to range the dreary sky:
Till down the eastern cliffs afar
Hyperion's march they spy and glittering shafts of war.

II.   2

  In climes beyond the solar road,
Where shaggy forms o'er ice-built mountains roam,   55
The Muse has broke the twilight-gloom
To cheer the shivering native's dull abode.
And oft beneath the odorous shade,
Of Chile's boundless forests laid,
She deigns to hear the savage youth repeat   60
In loose numbers wildly sweet
Their feather-cinctured chiefs and dusky loves.
Her track, where'er the goddess roves,
Glory pursue and generous Shame,
The unconquerable Mind and Freedom's holy flame.   65

II.   3

  Woods that wave o'er Delphi's steep,
Isles that crown the Aegean deep,
Fields that cool Ilissus laves,
Or where Maeander's amber waves
In lingering lab'rinths creep,   70
How do your tuneful echoes languish,
Mute but to the voice of anguish?
Where each old poetic mountain
Inspiration breathed around:
Every shade and hallowed fountain   75
Murmured deep a solemn sound:
Till the sad Nine in Greece's evil hour
Left their Parnassus for the Latian plains.
Alike they scorn the pomp of tyrant-power,
And coward Vice that revels in her chains.   80

When Latium had her lofty spirit lost,
They sought, oh Albion! next thy sea-encircled coast.

III.   1

Far from the sun and summer-gale,
In thy green lap was Nature's darling laid,
What time, where lucid Avon strayed,   85
To him the mighty Mother did unveil
Her awful face: the dauntless child
Stretched forth his little arms and smiled.
'This pencil take,' (she said) 'whose colours clear
Richly paint the vernal year: 90
Thine too these golden keys, immortal boy!
This can unlock the gates of joy;
Of horror that and thrilling fears,
Or ope the sacred source of sympathetic tears.'

III.   2

Nor second he, that rode sublime   95
Upon the seraph-wings of Ecstasy,
The secrets of the abyss to spy.
He passed the flaming bounds of place and time:
The living throne, the sapphire-blaze,
Where angels tremble while they gaze,   100
He saw; but blasted with excess of light,
Closed his eyes in endless night.
Behold, where Dryden's less presumptuous car,
Wide o'er the fields of glory, bear
Two coursers of ethereal race,   105
With necks in thunder clothed, and long-resounding pace.

III.   3

Hark, his hands the lyre explore!
Bright-eyed Fancy hovering o'er

Scatters from her pictured urn
Thoughts that breathe and words that burn. 110
But ah! 'tis heard no more———
Oh! lyre divine, what daring spirit
Wakes thee now? Though he inherit
Nor the pride nor ample pinion,
That the Theban eagle bear 115
Sailing with supreme dominion
Through the azure deep of air:
Yet oft before his infant eyes would run
Such forms as glitter in the Muse's ray
With orient hues, unborrowed of the sun: 120
Yet shall he mount and keep his distant way
Beyond the limits of a vulgar fate,
Beneath the Good how far—but far above the Great.

The Bard
A Pindaric Ode

I.   1

'Ruin seize thee, ruthless king!
'Confusion on thy banners wait,
'Though fanned by Conquest's crimson wing
'They mock the air with idle state.
'Helm nor hauberk's twisted mail,
'Nor even thy virtues, tyrant, shall avail 5
'To save thy secret soul from nightly fears,
'From Cambria's curse, from Cambria's tears!'
Such were the sounds, that o'er the crested pride
Of the first Edward scattered wild dismay,
As down the steep of Snowdon's shaggy side 10
He wound with toilsome march his long array.

Stout Gloucester stood aghast in speechless trance:
'To arms!', cried Mortimer and couched his quivering
    lance.

I. 2

  On a rock, whose haughty brow   15
Frowns o'er old Conway's foaming flood,
Robed in the sable garb of woe,
With haggard eyes the poet stood;
(Loose his beard and hoary hair
Streamed, like a meteor, to the troubled air)   20
And, with a master's hand and prophet's fire,
Struck the deep sorrows of his lyre.
'Hark, how each giant-oak and desert cave
'Sighs to the torrent's awful voice beneath!
'O'er thee, oh king! their hundred arms they wave,   25
'Revenge on thee in hoarser murmurs breathe;
'Vocal no more, since Cambria's fatal day,
'To high-born Hoel's harp or soft Llewellyn's lay.

I. 3

  'Cold is Cadwallo's tongue,
'That hushed the stormy main: 30
'Brave Urien sleeps upon his craggy bed:
'Mountains, ye mourn in vain
'Modred, whose magic song
'Made huge Plinlimmon bow his cloud-topped head.
'On dreary Arvon's shore they lie,   35
'Smeared with gore and ghastly pale:
'Far, far aloof the affrighted ravens sail;
'The famished eagle screams and passes by.
'Dear lost companions of my tuneful art,
'Dear as the light that visits these sad eyes,   40
'Dear as the ruddy drops that warm my heart,

'Ye died amidst your dying country's cries—
'No more I weep. They do not sleep.
'On yonder cliffs, a grisly band,
'I see them sit, they linger yet,   45
'Avengers of their native land;
'With me in dreadful harmony they join,
'And weave with bloody hands the tissue of thy line.'

II.   I

   "Weave the warp and weave the woof,
"The winding-sheet of Edward's race.   50
"Give ample room and verge enough
"The characters of hell to trace.
"Mark the year and mark the night,
"When Severn shall re-echo with affright
"The shrieks of death, through Berkeley's roofs that   55
      ring,
"Shrieks of an agonizing King!
"She-wolf of France, with unrelenting fangs,
"That tear'st the bowels of thy mangled mate,
"From thee be born who o'er thy country hangs
"The scourge of heaven. What terrors round him wait!   60
"Amazement in his van, with Flight combined,
"And Sorrow's faded form, and Solitude behind.

II.   2

   "Mighty victor, mighty lord,
"Low on his funeral couch he lies!
"No pitying heart, no eye, afford   65
"A tear to grace his obsequies.
"Is the sable warrior fled?
"Thy son is gone. He rests among the dead.
"The swarm that in thy noon-tide beam were born?
"Gone to salute the rising morn.   70

79

"Fair laughs the morn and soft the zephyr blows,
"While proudly riding o'er the azure realm
"In gallant trim the gilded vessel goes;
"Youth on the prow and Pleasure at the helm;
"Regardless of the sweeping whirlwind's sway,   75
"That, hushed in grim repose, expects his evening-prey.

II.   3

  "Fill high the sparkling bowl,
"The rich repast prepare,
"Reft of a crown, he yet may share the feast:
"Close by the regal chair   80
"Fell Thirst and Famine scowl
"A baleful smile upon their baffled guest.
"Heard ye the din of battle bray,
"Lance to lance and horse to horse?
"Long years of havoc urge their destined course, 85
"And through the kindred squadrons mow their way.
"Ye towers of Julius, London's lasting shame,
"With many a foul and midnight murther fed,
"Revere his consort's faith, his father's fame,
"And spare the meek usurper's holy head.   90
"Above, below, the rose of snow,
"Twined with her blushing foe, we spread:
"The bristled Boar in infant-gore
"Wallows beneath the thorny shade.
"Now, brothers, bending o'er the accursed loom,   95
"Stamp we our vengeance deep and ratify his doom.

III.   I

  "Edward, lo! to sudden fate
"(Weave we the woof. The thread is spun)
"Half of thy heart we consecrate.
"(The web is wove. The work is done.)"   100

'Stay, oh stay! nor thus forlorn
'Leave me unblessed, unpitied, here to mourn;
'In yon bright track, that fires the western skies,
'They melt, they vanish from my eyes.
'But oh! what solemn scenes on Snowdon's height   105
'Descending slow their glittering skirts unroll?
'Visions of glory, spare my aching sight,
'Ye unborn ages, crowd not on my soul!
'No more our long-lost Arthur we bewail.
'All-hail, ye genuine kings, Britannia's issue, hail!   110

III.   2

'Girt with many a baron bold
'Sublime their starry fronts they rear;
'And gorgeous dames, and statesmen old
'In bearded majesty, appear.
'In the midst a form divine!   115
'Her eye proclaims her of the Briton-line;
'Her lion-port, her awe-commanding face,
'Attempered sweet to virgin-grace.
'What strings symphonious tremble in the air,
'What strains of vocal transport round her play!   120
'Hear from the grave, great Taliessin, hear;
'They breathe a soul to animate thy clay.
'Bright Rapture calls and, soaring as she sings,
'Waves in the eye of heaven her many-coloured wings.

III.   3

'The verse adorn again   125
'Fierce war and faithful love,
'And truth severe, by fairy fiction dressed.
'In buskined measures move
'Pale Grief and pleasing Pain,
'With Horror, tyrant of the throbbing breast.   130

'A voice as of the cherub-choir
'Gales from blooming Eden bear;
'And distant warblings lessen on my ear,
'That lost in long futurity expire.
'Fond impious man, think'st thou yon sanguine cloud,   135
'Raised by thy breath, has quenched the orb of day?
'Tomorrow he repairs the golden flood,
'And warms the nations with redoubled ray.
'Enough for me: with joy I see
'The different doom our fates assign.   140
'Be thine despair and sceptered care;
'To triumph, and to die, are mine.'
He spoke, and headlong from the mountain's height
Deep in the roaring tide he plunged to endless night.

Ode on the Pleasure Arising from Vicissitude

Now the golden Morn aloft
Waves her dew-bespangled wing;
With vermeil cheek and whisper soft
She wooes the tardy spring,
Till April starts, and calls around   5
The sleeping fragrance from the ground;
And lightly o'er the living scene
Scatters his freshest, tenderest green.

New-born flocks in rustic dance
Frisking ply their feeble feet;   10
Forgetful of their wintry trance
The birds his presence greet:
But chief the sky-lark warbles high
His trembling thrilling ecstasy

And, lessening from the dazzled sight,   15
Melts into air and liquid light.

Yesterday the sullen year
Saw the snowy whirlwind fly;
Mute was the music of the air,
The herd stood drooping by: 20
Their raptures now that wildly flow,
No yesterday nor morrow know;
'Tis man alone that joy descries
With forward and reverted eyes.

Smiles on past Misfortune's brow   25
Soft Reflection's hand can trace;
And o'er the cheek of Sorrow throw
A melancholy grace;
While Hope prolongs our happier hour,
Or deepest shades, that dimly lower   30
And blacken round our weary way,
Gilds with a gleam of distant day.

Still, where rosy Pleasure leads,
See a kindred Grief pursue;
Behind the steps that Misery treads,   35
Approaching Comfort view:
The hues of bliss more brightly glow,
Chastised by sabler tints of woe;
And blended form, with artful strife,
The strength and harmony of life.   40

See the wretch, that long has tossed
On the thorny bed of pain,
At length repair his vigour lost,
And breathe and walk again:
The meanest flowret of the vale,   45

The simplest note that swells the gale,
The common sun, the air and skies,
To him are opening Paradise.

Humble Quiet builds her cell
Near the source whence Pleasure flows;   50
She eyes the clear crystalline well
And tastes it as it goes.
Far below   the crowd.
Broad and turbulent it grows
          with restless sweep   55
They perish in the boundless deep

Mark where Indolence and Pride,
Softly rolling side by side,
Their dull but daily round.

Epitaph on Mrs Clerke

Lo! where this silent marble weeps,
A friend, a wife, a mother sleeps:
A heart, within whose sacred cell
The peaceful virtues loved to dwell.
Affection warm, and faith sincere,   5
And soft humanity were there.
In agony, in death, resigned,
She felt the wound she left behind.
Her infant image, here below,
Sits smiling on a father's woe: 10
Whom what awaits, while yet he strays
Along the lonely vale of days?
A pang, to secret sorrow dear;

A sigh; an unavailing tear;
Till time shall every grief remove,   15
With life, with memory, and with love.

Epitaph on a Child

Here, freed from pain, secure from misery, lies
A child, the darling of his parents' eyes:
A gentler lamb ne'er sported on the plain,
A fairer flower will never bloom again.
Few were the days allotted to his breath;
Now let him sleep in peace his night of death.

The Fatal Sisters
An Ode

PREFACE

In the eleventh century Sigurd, Earl of the Orkney
Islands, went with a fleet of ships and a considerable body
of troops into Ireland, to the assistance of Sictryg with the
silken beard, who was then making war on his father-in-law
Brian, King of Dublin: the Earl and all his forces were cut   5
to pieces, and Sictryg was in danger of a total defeat; but
the enemy had a greater loss by the death of Brian, their
King, who fell in the action. On Christmas-day (the
day of the battle), a native of Caithness in Scotland saw at a
distance a number of persons on horseback riding full   10
speed towards a hill, and seeming to enter into it. Curiosity
led him to follow them, till looking through an opening
in the rocks he saw twelve gigantic figures resembling

women: they were all employed about a loom; and as they wove, they sung the following dreadful song; which when they had finished, they tore the web into twelve pieces, and (each taking her portion) galloped six to the north and as many to the south.

Now the storm begins to lower,
(Haste, the loom of hell prepare,)
Iron-sleet of arrowy shower
Hurtles in the darkened air.

Glittering lances are the loom,
Where the dusky warp we strain,
Weaving many a soldier's doom,
Orkney's woe, and Randver's bane.

See the grisly texture grow,
('Tis of human entrails made,)
And the weights that play below,
Each a gasping warrior's head.

Shafts for shuttles, dipped in gore,
Shoot the trembling cords along.
Sword, that once a monarch bore,
Keep the tissue close and strong!

Mista black, terrific maid,
Sangrida and Hilda see,
Join the wayward work to aid:
'Tis the woof of victory.

Ere the ruddy sun be set,
Pikes must shiver, javelins sing,
Blade with clattering buckler meet,
Hauberk crash and helmet ring.

(Weave the crimson web of war)   25
Let us go and let us fly,
Where our friends the conflict share,
Where they triumph, where they die.

As the paths of fate we tread,
Wading through the ensanguined field: 30
Gondula and Geira, spread
O'er the youthful King your shield.

We the reins to slaughter give,
Ours to kill and ours to spare:
Spite of danger he shall live.   35
(Weave the crimson web of war.)

They, whom once the desert-beach
Pent within its bleak domain,
Soon their ample sway shall stretch
O'er the plenty of the plain.   40

Low the dauntless Earl is laid,
Gored with many a gaping wound:
Fate demands a nobler head;
Soon a King shall bite the ground.

Long his loss shall Eirin weep,   45
Ne'er again his likeness see;
Long her strains in sorrow steep,
Strains of immortality!

Horror covers all the heath,
Clouds of carnage blot the sun.   50
Sisters, weave the web of death;
Sisters, cease. The work is done.

Hail the task, and hail the hands!
Songs of joy and triumph sing!
Joy to the victorious bands; 55
Triumph to the younger King.

Mortal, thou that hear'st the tale,
Learn the tenor of our song.
Scotland, through each winding vale
Far and wide the notes prolong. 60

Sisters, hence with spurs of speed:
Each her thundering faulchion wield;
Each bestride her sable steed.
Hurry, hurry to the field.

The Descent of Odin
An Ode

Uprose the King of Men with speed,
And saddled straight his coal-black steed;
Down the yawning steep he rode,
That leads to Hela's drear abode.
Him the dog of darkness spied, 5
His shaggy throat he opened wide,
While from his jaws, with carnage filled,
Foam and human gore distilled:
Hoarse he bays with hideous din,
Eyes that glow and fangs that grin; 10
And long pursues with fruitless yell
The father of the powerful spell.
Onward still his way he takes,
(The groaning earth beneath him shakes,)
Till full before his fearless eyes 15
The portals nine of hell arise.

Right against the eastern gate,
By the moss-grown pile he sate,
Where long of yore to sleep was laid
The dust of the prophetic maid.   20
Facing to the northern clime,
Thrice he traced the runic rhyme;
Thrice pronounced, in accents dread,
The thrilling verse that wakes the dead;
Till from out the hollow ground   25
Slowly breathed a sullen sound.

Pr. What call unknown, what charms, presume
To break the quiet of the tomb?
Who thus afflicts my troubled sprite,
And drags me from the realms of night?   30
Long on these mouldering bones have beat
The winter's snow, the summer's heat,
The drenching dews, and driving rain!
Let me, let me sleep again.
Who is he, with voice unblest,   35
That calls me from the bed of rest?

O. A Traveller, to thee unknown,
Is he that calls, a Warrior's son.
Thou the deeds of light shalt know;
Tell me what is done below,   40
For whom yon glittering board is spread,
Dressed for whom yon golden bed.

Pr. Mantling in the goblet see
The pure beverage of the bee,
O'er it hangs the shield of gold;   45
'Tis the drink of Balder bold:
Balder's head to death is given.
Pain can reach the sons of Heaven!

Unwilling I my lips unclose:
Leave me, leave me to repose. 50

O. Once again my call obey.
Prophetess, arise and say,
What dangers Odin's child await,
Who the author of his fate.

Pr. In Hoder's hand the hero's doom: 55
His brother sends him to the tomb.
Now my weary lips I close:
Leave me, leave me to repose.

O. Prophetess, my spell obey,
Once again arise and say, 60
Who the avenger of his guilt,
By whom shall Hoder's blood be spilt.

Pr. In the caverns of the west,
By Odin's fierce embrace compressed,
A wondrous boy shall Rinda bear, 65
Who ne'er shall comb his raven-hair,
Nor wash his visage in the stream,
Nor see the sun's departing beam:
Till he on Hoder's corse shall smile
Flaming on the funeral pile. 70
Now my weary lips I close:
Leave me, leave me to repose.

O. Yet a while my call obey.
Prophetess, awake and say,
What virgins these, in speechless woe, 75
That bend to earth their solemn brow,
That their flaxen tresses tear,
And snowy veils, that float in air.

Tell me whence their sorrows rose:
Then I leave thee to repose.   80

Pr. Ha! no Traveller art thou,
King of Men, I know thee now,
Mightiest of a mighty line——

O. No boding maid of skill divine
Art thou, nor prophetess of good;   85
But mother of the giant-brood!

Pr. Hie thee hence and boast at home,
That never shall enquirer come
To break my iron-sleep again,
Till Lok has burst his tenfold chain;   90
Never, till substantial Night
Has reassumed her ancient right;
Till wrapped in flames, in ruin hurled,
Sinks the fabric of the world.

The Triumphs of Owen
A Fragment

Owen's praise demands my song,
Owen swift, and Owen strong;
Fairest flower of Roderic's stem,
Gwyneth's shield and Britain's gem.
He nor heaps his brooded stores,   5
Nor on all profusely pours;
Lord of every regal art,
Liberal hand and open heart.

Big with hosts of mighty name,
Squadrons three against him came;   10
This the force of Eirin hiding;
Side by side as proudly riding,
On her shadow long and gay
Lochlin ploughs the watery way;
There the Norman sails afar   15
Catch the winds and join the war:
Black and huge along they sweep,
Burthens of the angry deep.

Dauntless on his native sands
The Dragon-son of Mona stands;   20
In glittering arms and glory dressed,
High he rears his ruby crest.
There the thundering strokes begin,
There the press and there the din;
Talymalfra's rocky shore   25
Echoing to the battle's roar.
Where his glowing eye-balls turn,
Thousand banners round him burn.
Where he points his purple spear,
Hasty, hasty Rout is there,   30
Marking with indignant eye
Fear to stop and shame to fly.
There Confusion, Terror's child,
Conflict fierce and Ruin wild,
Agony that pants for breath,   35
Despair and honourable Death.

The Death of Hoel

Had I but the torrent's might,
With headlong rage and wild affright

Upon Deïra's squadrons hurled,
To rush and sweep them from the world!
   Too, too secure in youthful pride,   5
By them my friend, my Hoël, died,
Great Cian's son: of Madoc old
He asked no heaps of hoarded gold;
Alone in nature's wealth arrayed,
He asked and had the lovely maid.   10
   To Cattraeth's vale in glittering row
Twice two hundred warriors go;
Every warrior's manly neck
Chains of regal honour deck,
Wreathed in many a golden link: 15
From the golden cup they drink
Nectar, that the bees produce,
Or the grape's ecstatic juice.
Flushed with mirth and hope they burn:
But none from Cattraeth's vale return,   20
Save Aeron brave and Conan strong,
(Bursting through the bloody throng)
And I, the meanest of them all,
That live to weep and sing their fall.

Caradoc

Have ye seen the tusky boar,
Or the bull, with sullen roar,
On surrounding foes advance?
So Caradoc bore his lance.

Conan

Conan's name, my lay, rehearse,
Build to him the lofty verse,
Sacred tribute of the bard,
Verse, the hero's sole reward.
As the flame's devouring force;   5
As the whirlwind in its course;
As the thunder's fiery stroke,
Glancing on the shivered oak;
Did the sword of Conan mow
The crimson harvest of the foe.   10

Sketch of his Own Character

Too poor for a bribe and too proud to importune,
He had not the method of making a fortune:
Could love and could hate, so was thought somewhat odd;
No very great wit, he believed in a God.
A post or a pension he did not desire,   5
But left church and state to Charles Townshend and Squire.

Epitaph on Sir William Williams

Here, foremost in the dangerous paths of fame,
Young Williams fought for England's fair renown;
His mind each Muse, each Grace adorned his frame,

Nor Envy dared to view him with a frown.
    At Aix uncalled his maiden sword he drew,   5
(There first in blood his infant glory sealed);
From fortune, pleasure, science, love, he flew,
And scorned repose when Britain took the field.
    With eyes of flame and cool intrepid breast,
Victor he stood on Belle Isle's rocky steeps;   10
Ah gallant youth! this marble tells the rest,
Where melancholy Friendship bends and weeps.

Song I ('Midst beauty and pleasure's gay triumphs to languish')

'Midst beauty and pleasure's gay triumphs, to languish
And droop without knowing the source of my anguish;
To start from short slumbers and look for the morning—
Yet close my dull eyes when I see it returning;

Sighs sudden and frequent, looks ever dejected,   5
Sounds that steal from my tongue, by no meaning
    connected!
Ah say, fellow-swains, how these symptoms befell me?
They smile, but reply not. Sure Delia will tell me!

Song II ('Thyrsis, when we parted, swore')

Thyrsis, when we parted, swore
Ere the spring he would return.
Ah, what means yon violet flower,
And the buds that deck the thorn?

'Twas the lark that upward sprung!   5
'Twas the nightingale that sung!
  Idle notes, untimely green,
  Why such unavailing haste?
Western gales and skies serene
Prove not always winter past.   10
Cease my doubts, my fears to move;
Spare the honour of my love.

The Candidate

When sly Jemmy Twitcher had smugged up his face
With a lick of court whitewash and pious grimace,
A-wooing he went, where three sisters of old
In harmless society guttle and scold.

  'Lord! Sister,' says Physic to Law, 'I declare   5
Such a sheep-biting look, such a pick-pocket air,
Not I, for the Indies! you know I'm no prude;
But his nose is a shame and his eyes are so lewd!
Then he shambles and straddles so oddly, I fear—
No; at our time of life, 'twould be silly, my dear.' 10
  'I don't know,' says Law, 'now methinks, for his look,
'Tis just like the picture in Rochester's book.
But his character, Phyzzy, his morals, his life;
When she died, I can't tell, but he once had a wife.

  'They say he's no Christian, loves drinking and   15
      whoring,
And all the town rings of his swearing and roaring,
His lying and filching, and Newgate-bird tricks:—
Not I,—for a coronet, chariot and six.'
  Divinity heard, between waking and dozing,
Her sisters denying and Jemmy proposing;   20

96

From dinner she rose with her bumper in hand,
She stroked up her belly and stroked down her band.
  'What a pother is here about wenching and roaring!
Why David loved catches and Solomon whoring.
Did not Israel filch from the Egyptians of old   25
Their jewels of silver and jewels of gold?
The prophet of Bethel, we read, told a lie;
He drinks: so did Noah; he swears: so do I.
To refuse him for such peccadillos were odd;
Besides, he repents, and he talks about God.   30
  'Never hang down your head, you poor penitent elf!
Come, buss me, I'll be Mrs Twitcher myself.
Damn ye both for a couple of Puritan bitches!
He's Christian enough that repents and that stitches.'

William Shakespeare to Mrs Anne, Regular Servant to the Revd Mr Precentor of York

  A moment's patience, gentle Mistress Anne!
  (But stint your clack for sweet St Charitie)
  'Tis Willy begs, once a right proper man,
Though now a book and interleaved, you see.
  Much have I borne from cankered critic's spite,   5
  From fumbling baronets and poets small,
Pert barristers and parsons nothing bright:
But what awaits me now is worst of all.
  'Tis true, our master's temper natural
  Was fashioned fair in meek and dovelike guise;   10
But may not honey's self be turned to gall
By residence, by marriage, and sore eyes?
  If then he wreak on me his wicked will,
Steal to his closet at the hour of prayer,

And (when thou hear'st the organ piping shrill) 15
Grease his best pen, and all he scribbles, tear.
  Better to bottom tarts and cheesecakes nice,
Better the roast meat from the fire to save,
Better be twisted into caps for spice,
Than thus be patched and cobbled in one's grave. 20
  So York shall taste what Clouët never knew,
So from *our* works sublimer fumes shall rise:
While Nancy earns the praise to Shakespeare due
For glorious puddings and immortal pies.

Epitaph on Mrs Mason

Tell them, though 'tis an awful thing to die,
('Twas e'en to thee) yet the dread path once trod,
Heaven lifts its everlasting portals high,
And bids the pure in heart behold their God.

Parody on an Epitaph

Now clean, now hideous, mellow now, now gruff,
She swept, she hissed, she ripened and grew rough,
At Broom, Pendragon, Appleby and Brough.

Invitation to Mason

Prim Hurd attends your call and Palgrave proud,
Stonhewer the lewd and Delaval the loud.
For thee does Powell squeeze and Marriott sputter,

And Glynn cut phizzes and Tom Nevile stutter.
Brown sees thee sitting on his nose's tip,   5
The Widow feels thee in her aching hip,
For thee fat Nanny sighs and handy Nelly,
And Balguy with a bishop in his belly!

On L[or]d H[olland']s Seat near M[argat]e, K[en]t

Old and abandoned by each venal friend,
　Here H[olland] took the pious resolution
To smuggle some few years and strive to mend
　A broken character and constitution.
On this congenial spot he fixed his choice;   5
　Earl Godwin trembled for his neighbouring sand;
Here sea-gulls scream and cormorants rejoice,
　And mariners, though shipwrecked, dread to land.
Here reign the blustering North and blighting East,
　No tree is heard to whisper, bird to sing: 10
Yet nature cannot furnish out the feast,
　Art he invokes new horrors still to bring.
Now mouldering fanes and battlements arise,
　Arches and turrets nodding to their fall,
Unpeopled palaces delude his eyes,   15
　And mimic desolation covers all.
'Ah'. said the sighing peer, 'had Bute been true
　Nor Shelburne's, Rigby's, Calcraft's friendship vain,
Far other scenes than these had blessed our view
　And realised the ruins that we feign.   20
Purged by the sword and beautified by fire,
　Then had we seen proud London's hated walls:
Owls might have hooted in St Peter's choir,
　And foxes stunk and littered in St Paul's.'

Ode for Music

'Hence, avaunt, ('tis holy ground)
'Comus and his midnight-crew,
'And Ignorance with looks profound,
'And dreaming Sloth of pallid hue,
'Mad Sedition's cry profane,   5
'Servitude that hugs her chain,
'Nor in these consecrated bowers
'Let painted Flattery hide her serpent-train in flowers.

Chorus

'Nor Envy base nor creeping Gain
'Dare the Muse's walk to stain.   10
'While bright-eyed Science watches round:
'Hence, away, 'tis holy ground!'

Recitative

From yonder realms of empyrean day
Bursts on my ear the indignant lay:
There sit the sainted sage, the bard divine,   15
The few whom genius gave to shine
Through every unborn age and undiscovered clime.
Rapt in celestial transport they,   (*accomp.*)
Yet hither oft a glance from high
They send of tender sympathy   20
To bless the place, where on their opening soul
First the genuine ardour stole.
'Twas Milton struck the deep-toned shell,

And, as the choral warblings round him swell,
Meek Newton's self bends from his state sublime,   25
And nods his hoary head and listens to the rhyme.

Air

'Ye brown o'er-arching groves,
'That Contemplation loves,
'Where willowy Camus lingers with delight!
'Oft at the blush of dawn   30
'I trod your level lawn,
'Oft wooed the gleam of Cynthia silver-bright
'In cloisters dim, far from the haunts of Folly,
'With Freedom by my side, and soft-eyed Melancholy.'

Recitative

But hark! the portals sound and, pacing forth   35
With solemn steps and slow,
High potentates and dames of royal birth
And mitred fathers in long order go:
Great Edward with the lilies on his brow
From haughty Gallia torn,   40
And sad Chatillon, on her bridal morn
That wept her bleeding love, and princely Clare,
And Anjou's heroine, and the paler rose,
The rival of her crown and of her woes,
And either Henry there,   45
The murthered saint and the majestic lord,
That broke the bonds of Rome,
(Their tears, their little triumphs o'er,   (*accomp.*)
Their human passions now no more,
Save charity, that glows beyond the tomb).   50
All that on Granta's fruitful plain
Rich streams of regal bounty poured,
And bade these awful fanes and turrets rise,
To hail their Fitzroy's festal morning come;

101

And thus they speak in soft accord   55
The liquid language of the skies.

'What is grandeur, what is power?
'Heavier toil, superior pain.
'What the bright reward we gain?
'The grateful memory of the good.   60
'Sweet is the breath of vernal shower,
'The bee's collected treasures sweet,
'Sweet music's melting fall, but sweeter yet
'The still small voice of gratitude.'

Recitative

Foremost and leaning from her golden cloud   65
The venerable Margaret see!
'Welcome, my noble son,' (she cries aloud)
'To this, thy kindred train, and me:
'Pleased in thy lineaments we trace
'A Tudor's fire, a Beaufort's grace.   70

Air

'Thy liberal heart, thy judging eye,
'The flower unheeded shall descry,
'And bid it round heaven's altars shed
'The fragrance of its blushing head:
'Shall raise from earth the latest gem   75
'To glitter on the diadem.

Recitative

'Lo, Granta waits to lead her blooming band,
'Not obvious, not obtrusive, she
'No vulgar praise, no venal incense flings;
'Nor dares with courtly tongue refined   80
'Profane thy inborn royalty of mind:

'She reveres herself and thee.
'With modest pride to grace thy youthful brow
'The laureate wreath, that Cecil wore, she brings,
'And to thy just, thy gentle hand   85
'Submits the fasces of her sway,
'While spirits blest above and men below
'Join with glad voice the loud symphonius lay.

Grand Chorus
'Through the wild waves as they roar
'With watchful eye and dauntless mien   90
'Thy steady course of honour keep,
'Nor fear the rocks nor seek the shore:
'The star of Brunswick smiles serene,
'And gilds the horrors of the deep.'

Verse Fragments

Gratitude
    The Joy that trembles in her eye
    She bows her meek & humble head
          in silent praise
      beyond the power of Sound.
(Mr Pope dead)
    and smart beneath the visionary scourge
    —'tis Ridicule & not reproach that wounds
    Their vanity & not their conscience feels

    A few shall
    The cadence of my song repeat
    & hail thee in my words.

Impromptus

Extempore by **Mr Gr**[ay] on Dr K[eene], B[ishop] of C[hester]:
    The Bishop of Chester
    Though wiser than Nestor
    And fairer than Esther,
    If you scratch him will fester.

One day the Bishop having offered to give a gentleman a goose, Mr Gr[ay] composed his epitaph thus:

Here lies Edmund Keene Lord Bishop of Chester,
He eat a fat goose and could not digest her—

And this upon his lady:

Here lies Mrs Keene, the Bishop of Chester,
She had a bad face which did sadly molest her.

Impromptu by Mr Gray, going out of Raby Castle:

Here lives Harry Vane,
Very good claret and fine champagne.

A couplet by Mr Gray:

When you rise from your dinner as light as before,
'Tis a sign you have eat just enough and no more.

Couplet about Birds

There pipes the woodlark, and the song-thrush there
Scatters his loose notes in the waste of air.

Lines on Dr Robert Smith

Do you ask why old Focus Silvanus defies,
And leaves not a chestnut in being?
'Tis not that old Focus himself has got eyes,
But because he has writ about seeing.

Satire on the Heads of Houses;

or, Never a Barrel the Better Herring

O Cambridge, attend
To the satire I've penned
On the heads of thy Houses,
Thou seat of the Muses!
Know the Master of Jesus   5
Does hugely displease us;
The Master of Maudlin
In the same dirt is dawdling;
The Master of Sidney
Is of the same kidney;   10
The Master of Trinity
To him bears affinity;
As the Master of Keys
Is as like as two peas,
So the Master of Queen's   15
Is as like as two beans;
The Master of King's
Copies them in all things;
The Master of Catherine
Takes them all for his pattern;   20
The Master of Clare
Hits them all to a hair;
The Master of Christ
By the rest is enticed;
But the Master of Emmanuel   25
Follows them like a spaniel;
The Master of Benet
Is of the like tenet;

The Master of Pembroke
Has from them his system took;   30
The Master of Peter's
Has all the same features;
The Master of St John's
Like the rest of the dons.

P.S.—As to Trinity Hall
We say nothing at all.

COMMENTARY

p. 37   Lines Spoken by the Ghost of John Dennis at the Devil Tavern

This is Gray's earliest known poem in English. It was written on 8 December 1734 and sent to Horace Walpole. John Dennis (1657–1734) was a dramatist and critic, satirized by Pope who had also mentioned The Devil Tavern which was in Fleet Street. The literary genre of a dialogue from the dead had been established by Lucian.

1 *Elysian scene*: Elysium was the abode of departed souls in Greek mythology.

3 *Atropos*: the woman who severed the thread of life in Greek mythology.

4 *Celadon*: Walpole's name in the 'Quadruple Alliance'.

9 *Tartarean*: hellish.

13 An allusion to a famous poem by the Emperor Hadrian. The first of many such classical allusions in Gray's poetry.

23 *asphodel*: a plant sacred to Proserpine in Greek mythology.

25 *'Lysium*: Elysium, *vide supra*.

33 *Greensickness*: an anaemic disease affecting girls at puberty.

35 *Nicolini*: Nicolino Grimaldi, a popular castrato opera singer of the time.

39 *Proserpine*: mortal beloved of the god of the underworld. *Pluto*: lover of Proserpine.

41 *Orozmades*: one of Gray's names in the 'Quadruple Alliance'.

42 *Lucrece*: wife of Tarquin. Having confessed to being raped by Sextus she committed suicide.

43 *Mrs. Oldfield*: a famous actress and courtesan.

50 *Queen Artemisia*: a character in Rowe's *Ambitious Stepmother* who mixed ashes in her daily drink to mourn her husband. *bohea*: tea.

51 *ramilie*: a particularly elaborate wig unsuitable for such a conqueror.

p. 39   Agrippina, a Tragedy

This unfinished play was begun by Gray in the winter of 1741–1742 and was closely modelled on *Britannicus* which was his favourite play of Racine's which he had seen performed in Paris. Gray was uneasy about the length of the speeches, West about the diction. The plot, which would not have made for great tragedy, is taken from Tacitus.

5 *lictor*: an attendant who walked before Roman officials.
21 *aconite*: a poisonous plant.
30 *Jove*: chief of the gods.
40 *edileship*: the office of magistrate to the common people in ancient Rome.
50 *Julian*: of the house of Julius Caesar.
64 *Magi*: wise men.
99-100 *Rubellius* and *Sylla*: noblemen tempted to rebel for Agrippina.
115 *Praetorian camp*: the Praetorians were the imperial bodyguard.
117 *Juno*: the Roman goddess of women.
171 *Syllani*: brothers destroyed by Agrippina.

p. 47   Ode on the Spring
This poem is discussed in the Introduction, p. 8.

2 *Venus*: here the goddess of propagation.
5 *Attic*: Greek.
9 *zephyrs*: personifications of breezes.

p. 49   Ode on a Distant Prospect of Eton College
This poem is also discussed in the Introduction, p. 11. The epigraph is from Menander and may be translated: 'I am a man, a sufficient cause for being unhappy.'

3 *Science*: all aspects of knowledge.
4 *Henry*: Henry VI, founder of Eton College.
23 *margent green*: banks.
61-70 Such personifications are classical and derive largely from Virgil.
99-100 Although these are two of Gray's most famous lines, the idea has a history dating back at least as far as Sophocles.

p. 52   Sonnet on the Death of Mr Richard West
See Introduction, p. 10.

2 *Phoebus*: the sun.

p. 53   Ode to Adversity

See Introduction, p. 12. The epigraph to this poem is taken from Aeschylus and may be translated: 'Zeus, who leadeth mortals in the way of understanding, Zeus, who hath established as a fixed ordinance that wisdom comes by suffering.'

1 *Jove*: alternatively Zeus, chief of the gods.
5 *adamantine*: made of adamant, i.e. unbreakable.
35 *Gorgon*: a face circled with snakes like the Gorgon's.
36 *vengeful band*: presumably the Furies.

p. 55   Hymn to Ignorance

This poem is a satire on Cambridge.

3 *Camus*: personification of the river Cam in Cambridge, perhaps derived from Milton.
11 *Hyperion*: the sun.
14 *aegis*: shield.
17 *Lethean*: Lethe was one of the rivers of hell in classical mythology and produced forgetfulness.
37 *Sesostris*: a legendary Egyptian conqueror.

p. 56   Ode on the Death of a Favourite Cat

See Introduction, p. 25.

15 *genii*: local spirits.
16 *Tyrian*: purple.
34 *Nereid*: sea-nymph.

p. 58   The Alliance of Education and Government

The poem is discussed in the Introduction with reference to the Elegy. The epigraph from Theocritus reads: 'Begin, my friend, for in no way can you take your song with you to Hades that puts all things out of mind.'

77 *Zembla*: Nova Zembla, a group of islands in the Arctic Ocean.

p. 61   Tophet

This is a satire on the Rev. Henry Etough, rector of Therfield in Hertford-shire. He was a malicious gosssip and social climber whose periodic visits to Cambridge were always accompanied by trouble and emnity.

6 *proselyte*: a new convert.

p. 61   Elegy Written in a Country Churchyard

This is, of course, Gray's most famous poem and I have devoted a section of the Introduction (pp. 13–20 *ff.*) to discussing its content and implications.

5-8 These lines are very reminiscent of a stanza in Thomas Warton's second *Pastoral Eclogue*. Gray's lines are much superior and illustrate the advantages of a common poetic diction.

41 *storied*: inscribed or illustrated.

57 *Hampden*: a champion of civil liberty in the time of Charles I.

119 *Science*: knowledge in general.

124 Probably a reference to West.

p. 66   A Long Story

This poem was written while Gray was staying at Stoke Poges. Two friends of Lady Cobham, who lived nearby and was an admirer of the *Elegy*, were sent to seek the poet out. Gray hated publicity, but in this case he succumbed and was to be a great friend of one of these ladies – a certain Miss Speed.

3 The Huntingdons and Hattons had built the 'ancient pile' of the Manor House at Stoke Poges.

6 *achievements*: coats of arms.

11 Sir Christopher Hatton had been Queen Elizabeth's Lord Keeper. The seal and maces were the insignia of his office.

25 *cap-a-pee*: literally from head to foot. Gray probably refers to her clothes.

29 *Amazon*: a race of female warriors in Greek mythology.

31 *Cobham*: Lady Cobham, owner of the Manor House at Stoke Poges.

37 *capucine*: a hood with a cloak resembling the habit of a Capuchin monk.

41 *P——t*: Robert Purt who had told the ladies about Gray.

64 *tester*: canopy over a bed.

91 *Phoebus*: god of the sun and the Muses.

103 *Styack*: the housekeeper.

115 *Squib*: groom of the chambers.

116 *Groom*: the steward.

120 *Macleane*: a highwayman who had been hanged the week before.

133-40 These lines satirize the position of a mere poet in society.

142 *lubbers*: idle people.

144 *rubbers*: games of whist.

p. 72   Stanzas to Mr Bentley

Richard Bentley was responsible for the illustrations to the 1753 edition of Gray's poems published by Walpole. Gray admired the artist's work immensely but some reviewers considered these lines excessive.

26-28 The rhymes for these lines are missing in the manuscript. Considering Gray's practice of imitation, Mitford's idea that 'Gray had in his mind Dryden's Epistle to Kneller, from which he partly took his expressions' affords the most likely emendation:

> Enough for me, if to some feeling breast
> My lines a secret sympathy convey
> And as their pleasing influence is exprest
> A sigh of soft reflection dies away.

p. 73   The Progress of Poesy. A Pindaric Ode

I have dealt at length with this poem in the Introduction (p. 27). The epigraph from Pindar may be translated: 'vocal to the intelligent alone'.

1 *Aeolian*: a mode in Greek music. The line has its origin in Psalm lvii, 9 'Awake, my glory; awake, lute and harp.'

3 *Helicon*: the spring on Parnassus, the home of the Muses.

9 *Ceres*: goddess of the harvest.

17 *Thracia*: Thrace, a region famous for its fighting men.

27 *Idalia*: a town in Crete where Aphrodite was worshipped.

29 *Cythera*: the island where Aphrodite was born and by extension the goddess herself.

53 *Hyperion*: the sun.

62 *feather-cinctured*: wearing feather headresses.

66 *Delphi*: home of the oracle of Apollo.

68 *Ilissus*: a stream running through Athens.

69 *Maeander*: a particularly winding river.

77 *the sad Nine*: the Muses.

78 *Parnassus*: home of the Muses. *Latian*: ancient Roman.

85 The lines refer to Shakespeare.

95 The lines refer to Milton.

p. 77 The Bard. A Pindaric Ode

I have described the background to this poem in the Introduction, p. 31.

5 *hauberk*: 'The Hauberk was a texture of steel ringlets, or rings interwoven, forming a coat of mail, that sate close to the body, and adapted itself to every motion.' Gray's note in the 1768 edition.

8 *Cambria*: Wales.

14 *Mortimer*: a lord of the Welsh Marches and a powerful follower of the king.

28-33 These are Welsh names but not those of known bards.

55 Edward II was murdered in Berkeley Castle.

57 *She-wolf of France*: Isabel, Edward II's adulterous queen.

59 'Triumphs of Edward the Third in France'. Gray 1768.

64 Death of Edward III.

67 A reference to the Black Prince.

71 'Magnificence of Richard the Second's reign.' Gray's note.

83 'Ruinous civil wars of York and Lancaster.' Gray's note.

87 *towers of Julius*: the Tower of London.

90 *the meek usurper*: Henry VI.

91-92 'The white and red roses, devices of York and Lancaster.' Gray's note.

93 *The bristled Boar*: Richard III.

99 Eleanor of Castile, Edward's wife.

110 References to the Tudor dynasty who were Welsh in origin.

115 Elizabeth I.

121 *Taliessin*: 'Chief of the Bards, flourished in the VIth Centuary.' Gray's note.

126 A quotation from and reference to Spenser.

128 *buskined*: tragic, referring to the boot worn in Athenian tragedy.

131 Milton.

p. 82 Ode on the Pleasure Arising from Vicissitude

Gray began this uncompleted poem in 1754 or 55 and seems to have been inspired in part by a French poem called *Epitre à ma Soeur* by Gresset.

p. 84   Epitaph on Mrs Clerke

Gray wrote this poem not later than 1758 and described it as 'an epitaph on the Wife of a Friend of mine'. This friend was John Clerke, a contemporary of Gray's at Peterhouse. Mrs Clerke had died in childbirth in 1757.

p. 85   Epitaph on a Child

Written in 1758, the poem was inspired by the death of Robert, the son of Gray's close friend, Dr Thomas Wharton.

p. 85   The Fatal Sisters. An Ode

This free translation was associated with Gray's ambitious plans, never fully realized, of writing a history of English poetry. The Norse original concerns the Battle of Clontarf which was fought in 1014 and claims to be a prophetic account. I have discussed the importance of Gray's interest in Norse poetry in the Introduction. He took this poem from a Latin transcription.

8 *Orkney*: Earl Sigurd. *Randver's bane*: This is unclear in the original, but probably refers to Odin, the killer of Randver.
17 *Mista*: this and the following names are those of Valkyries who were described by Gray as 'female Divinities, Servants of *Odin* (or *Woden*) in Gothic mythology.

p. 88   The Descent of Odin. An Ode

The poem concerns the visit that Odin made, before the death of his son Balder, to the underworld. Here he was to learn the boy's fate. The prophetess identifies Hoder as the murderer and Odin's son Vali as the avenger.

4 *Hela's drear abode*: Hela was the goddess of death who sat at the gate of hell.
5 *dog*: Garm, guardian of the gate of hell.
65 *Rinda*: mother of the avenger Vali.
90 *Lok*: the spirit of evil who is bound until the end of the world.

p. 91 The Triumphs of Owen. A Fragment

Gray's note on this poem reads: 'Owen succeeded his Father Griffin in the Principality of North-Wales, a.d. 1120. This battle was fought near fourty years afterwards.'

3 *Roderic*: a prince who had divided Wales among his sons.
4 *Gwyneth*: North Wales.
15 *Norman*: Norwegian not French.
25 *Talymalfra*: a small bay in north-east Anglesey.

p. 92 The Death of Hoel

3 *Deïra*: a Saxon kingdom in Yorkshire.

p. 94 Sketch of his Own Character

6 *Townshend*: a Chancellor of the Exchequer.

p. 94 Epitaph on Sir William Williams

Gray was urged to write this poem by a mutual friend. He had known Williams, who had been killed at the siege of Belle Isle in Brittany, but slightly.

p. 95 Song I

This and the following song were written at the request of Miss Speed.

p. 96 The Candidate

This vitriolic poem, remarkable for Gray, was written in 1764. In that year the High Stewardship of Cambridge University fell free. The post had previously been held by a Whig, but now that that party had fallen from power it was proposed that a Tory, John Montague, fourth Earl of Sandwich, should be elected. The post was one of considerable patronage and influence, hence the political involvement. This patronage was particularly extensive in the Church, and the fact that Sandwich – the Jemmy Twitcher of the poem – was notoriously profligate yet widely supported by the Divinity Faculty is the central irony of Gray's poem.

4 *guttle*: gormandizing. *scold*: noisely argumentative.
12 The second Earl of Rochester was an ancestor of Sandwich's and a notorious libertine.
17 *Newgate-bird*: a prisoner at Newgate prison.
21 *bumper*: glass.
32 *buss*: kiss.

p. 97   William Shakespeare to Mrs Anne, Regular Servant to the Revd Precentor of York

Gray's friend Mason held the position of Precentor at York and was at this time, 1765, annotating Shakespeare.

p. 98   Parody on an Epitaph

This parodies an epitaph written by Anne Clifford on her mother, the Countess of Cumberland who resided consecutively at each of the castles mentioned in the last line.

p. 98   Invitation to Mason

This poem was included in a letter to Mason dated 8 January 1768 and lists various mutual friends.

1 *Hurd*: critic and writer of the influential *Letters on Chivalry and Romance*.
4 *cuts phizzes*: pulls grimaces.
6-7 These appear to be the names of serving women in Gray's coffee house.

p. 99   On L[or]d H[olland']s Seat near M[argat]e, K[en]t

Lord Holland had amassed a fortune in government service and had built a strange family seat at Margate, the grounds of which were cluttered with ruins and gave strange, contrived views.

6 *Earl Godwin*: a reference to the notorious Goodwin Sands which had belonged to Earl Godwine in the eleventh century.

p. 100 Ode for Music

This is Gray's last important poem. It was written for his patron the Duke of Grafton and was performed at his installation as Chancellor to the University in 1769. Gray composed it largely out of a sense of duty, for Grafton was responsible for obtaining for him the post of Regius Professor of History. Gray was uneasy both about the poem's merit and the flattery it contains.

2 *Comus*: spirit of wildness and laxity is Milton's poem.

30-34 A deliberate pastiche of *Il Penseroso*. Gray considered Milton to have been the most distinguished poet Cambridge had fostered.

39 A reference to Edward III, founder of Trinity College. The lilies were those of conquered France.

41 *Chatillon*: Mary, Countess of Pembroke and founder of a college of that name.

42 *Clare*: Elizabeth, Countess of Clare, another founder.

43 *Anjou*: Margaret of Anjou, founder of Queen's College. *paler rose*: Elizabeth Woodville who had extended the foundation of Queen's.

45 References to Henry VI and Henry VIII, one the founder of King's, the other the greatest benefactor of King's.

46 *saint*: Henry VI. *majestic lord*: Henry VIII.

51 *Granta*: a Cambridge river.

54 *Fitzroy*: Grafton himself.

66 *Margaret*: Countess of Richmond and Derby and founder of John's and Christ's Colleges.

70 Grafton claimed descent from both these families.

84 *Cecil*: William Cecil, Lord Burleigh, Elizabeth I's great minister had also been Chancellor of the university.

93 *Brunswick*: the ruling house of the day.

INDEX OF TITLES AND FIRST LINES